The
HUDSON RIVER:
Inspiration & Challenge

Bear Mountain Bridge

The HUDSON RIVER:
Inspiration & Challenge

A Conference on Contemporary Culture

ELIZABETH BEIRNE, Ph.D.
Editor

JAN L. MUNRO
Artist

The HUDSON RIVER: Inspiration & Challenge
Copyright © 1997
by The History of New York City Project, Inc.
All rights reserved. Printed in the United States of America.

Designer: Henry C. Meyer, Jr.

The HUDSON RIVER: Inspiration & Challenge
conference on contemporary culture was sponsored by

The Institute for Applied Philosophy
   College of Mount Saint Vincent.

The Bronx County Historical Society.

The History of New York City Project, Inc.

ISBN 0-9652331-1-1

Dr. Gary Hermalyn,
Project Director

Acknowledgement

The Mount Saint Vincent community is the source of inspiration and the foundation for the programs of the Institute for Applied Philosophy. The conference on which this book is based was conceived to provide a 'voice for the river' in keeping with the call of the Sisters of Charity. For one hundred and forty years the Sisters have been inspired by the Hudson's beauty and have cherished its shores. Today, under Sr. Elizabeth Vermaelen's tenure, their mission continues with vision and dedicated leadership. Several Sisters have stepped forth in support of this conference and the Institute's efforts to recognize the challenge and opportunity of this great resource. They include Sr. Theresa Capria, Sr. Margurite Caso, Sr. Carol Finegan, Sr. Mary Ann Garisto, Sr. Marion Hunt, Sr. Joseph McKevitt, and Sr. Margaret Sweeney. I would like to especially acknowledge the kind and astute guidance of Sr. Kathleen Gilbride. President Mary Stuart graciously welcomed everyone to the conference and provided the foreword to this volume.

My sincerest thanks to The Bronx County Historical Society for the services of its staff including Mrs. Kathleen Pacher, Ms. Catherine Pellicano, Mrs. Katherine Gleeson, Dr. Peter Derrick, and Dr. Gary Hermalyn, Executive Director of the Society. Ms. Jan Munro's lovely paintings of the Hudson River have made the book truly a work of art.

This book was made possible by the generous support of the History of New York City Project, Inc. and The Bronx County Historical Society. The Project funded the conference on which this volume is based and has pledged its continued support for the Institute's conferences leading up to the Greater New York City Centennial Celebration in 1998.

Elizabeth Beirne

Henry Hudson in 1609

Dedicated to

Cender and Tom
who crossed the river
many a time

Statue of Liberty

Contents

List of Illustrations xiii

List of Conference Speakers xv

Dr. Mary Stuart
Foreword.. xix

Dr. Elizabeth Beirne
Introduction xxiii

Mr. Thomas Brosnan
History of Water Pollution in the Hudson River 1

Ms. Cathy Drew
The River Environment 11

Dr. Peter Derrick
Crossing the Hudson... 21

Dr. Allan S. Gilbert
Archaeology in the Hudson Valley 35

Mr. Robert Kornfeld
Hudson River Architecture 61

Ms. Tema Harnik
Historic Hudson Valley 71

Ms. Mary Siobhan Sullivan
What We Say When We Write About the River 79

Mr. Wilbur Woods
Planning for New York's Waterfront 89

Index 96

Biographies of the Speakers 100

Hayride Near Rip Van Winkle Bridge

List of Illustrations

Bear Mountain Bridge..................... Opposite Title Page

Henry Hudson in 1609 viii

Statue of Liberty x

Hayride Near Rip Van Winkle Bridge.......................xii

Sleepy Hollow xiv

Ice Skaters..xvi

Fonthill Castle, The Bronx xviii

Tarrytown Lighthouse...............................xxi

Spuyten Duyvil xxii

Tappan Zee xxvii

Harlem River Ship Canal..............................xxviii

Ice Harvesting 9

The River Project Pier 10

Storm King..19

Staten Island Ferry 20

Proposed New Rail Line Across Hudson (map).............. 31

Albany 33

William Underhill Brickyard...........................34

Bricks of the Hudson River Valley (photograph).............. 53

West Point...59

Sunnyside...60

Esopus Lighthouse 69

Kykuit..70

Indian Village......................................77

College of Mount Saint Vincent.........................78

Rip Van Winkle 87

Chelsea Piers.......................................88

West Shore Railroad 95

Old Dutch Farm 99

Palisades..102

Reading Along the River...............................105

Sleepy Hollow

THE HUDSON RIVER:
INSPIRATION AND CHALLENGE

A Conference on Contemporary Culture

April 20, 1996

SPEAKERS:

Dr. Mary Stuart
President, College of Mount Saint Vincent

Mr. Thomas Brosnan
Chief, Marine Sciences Section,
NYC Department of Environmental Protection

Ms. Cathy Drew
Director, The River Project

Dr. Peter Derrick
Manager of Long Range Planning,
Metropolitan Transportation Authority

Dr. Allan S. Gilbert
Associate Professor of Anthropology
Archaeological Director, Rose Hill Manor Project
Fordham University

Mr. Robert Kornfeld
Chairman, Riverdale Historic District
Co-Author, *Landmarks of The Bronx*

Ms. Tema Harnick
Administrative Consultant, Lower Hudson
Conference of Historical Agencies and Museums

Ms. Mary Siobhan Sullivan
Visiting Instructor of English,
College of Mount Saint Vincent

Mr. Wilbur L. Woods
Director, Waterfront and Open Space Division
NYC Department of City Planning

MODERATOR:

Dr. Elizabeth Beirne
Associate Professor, Philosophy
Director, The Institute for Applied Philosophy
College of Mount Saint Vincent

Ice Skaters

The
HUDSON RIVER:
Inspiration & Challenge

Forthill Castle, The Bronx

DR. MARY STUART

Foreword

ON BEHALF of the College of Mount Saint Vincent, I'd like to welcome all of you to our view and our experience of the Hudson River in spring.

When I first came here to the College, our students, alumnae, alumni, faculty and staff, all told me that I would be captured by the river. I didn't exactly know what they meant by that, but now I understand. My office is next to this room and, in fact, looks out over the Hudson with its incredible sights like the immense tankers that glide by. It really is remarkable and reminds me, of course, of how critical the river still is to commerce.

Then, in the summer, I get to see the small, bobbing sailboats, and at that point they call to me to be out on the river and enjoying that beautiful peacefulness as well as the beauty of the Palisades. Around here, you can see the migrating birds which, again, shows that even in this incredible urban sprawl of New York City we have a bit of the undomesticated, uncultivated wild river environment. What fascinates me most is during the wintertime as I watch the icepacks flow down the river, but, also almost incredibly, up the river.

So – I have in fact been captured by the river. I think also the presence of the Hudson so near to this college has affected the educational and the life experience of all of us who live in this community. It is a part of us, and it is important, if you will, to who we are, even while we don't speak of it so much in that way. In closing, I must say I'm really pleased that The Institute for Applied Philosophy here at the College, is sponsoring this really wonderful, wonderful day. The river is a part of our past, certainly of our present, and also of our future. This is true for all of us collectively – all of us who share in the river.

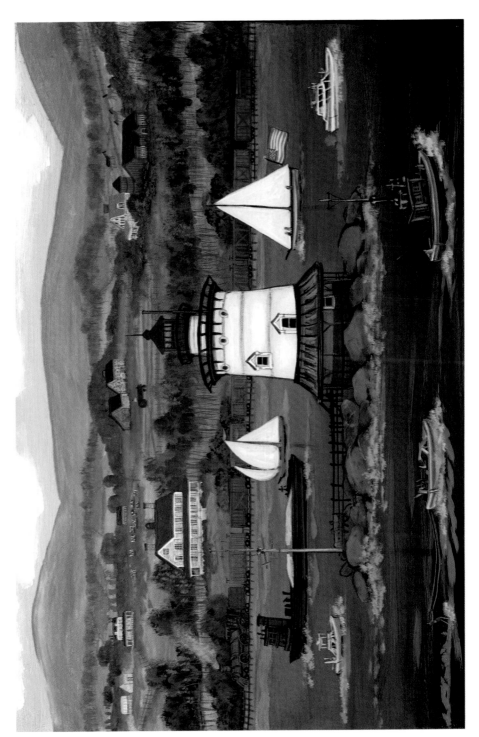

Tarrytown Lighthouse

Spuyten Duyvil

DR. ELIZABETH BEIRNE

Introduction

THE ARTICLES in this book were originally presented at the annual spring conference of The Institute for Applied Philosophy at the College of Mount Saint Vincent. This series of conferences and books is produced by the Institute in collaboration with The History of New York City Project, Inc. The aim is to set the scene for the centennial celebrations of the incorporation of Greater New York City in 1998.

The Institute for Applied Philosophy was conceived to provide a forum for creative insight in the problems that face us at the close of this millennium. Here specialists can enlarge their vision by sharing perspectives with others from diverse disciplines as we explore the role the Hudson River has played in the New York City area and its challenges for the future. The environmental issues are addressed by governmental officials and representatives from non-profit groups. The social and natural history is revealed by historians and anthropologists. Future plans for the river are discussed by regional planners. The role of a river as an inspiration and metaphor is explored by a literary scholar and architectural historians.

This time last year our conference theme was *New York City at the Turn of the Century*. It was the consensus of the speakers then that the city was still necessary despite the overwhelming information revolution that is connecting us via technology. Although we have the ability to be connected globally from our homes we need to have face-to-face encounters and that's what we are doing here today. We are meeting and greeting each other and reflecting from our various points of view on this mighty force of nature at our doorstep. So we will begin to relate our different versions of the Hudson River.

I am reminded, when I think of the river, of the first philosopher. Thales lived in the sixth century B.C. in what was called Greece but today is modern Turkey. He lived on a peninsula jutting out where the Aegean Sea and the Mediterranean Sea join. He was very affected by his travels and encounters with travelers from all over the world of his day, which included Syria, Israel, Egypt and Persia, and also the rest of Greece. He was hearing a lot of stories, stories that told of the origins of the world and the way the world worked, but none of these stories seemed to fit together.

Thales' exposure to many different cultures led him to question the veracity of the myths offered to explain the world. All the conflicting religious versions could not be true, and Thales saw no reason why his native Greek version was any better than the others. He turned from mythological explanation and, as an engineer, was inclined to seek the answer in a logical theory, in the physical structure of nature.

Here on the shores of the Hudson, we can understand why Thales thought that "everything is water." He theorized that water was the most basic element because it could change its form from a liquid to a gas or to a solid. For the ancient Greeks this metamorphosis was miraculous, as they did not understand the process clearly and believed that water actually became something else, and thus could be transformed into the other elements, air, and earth. Everything alive seemed to need water and be largely composed of it. The Greek word for water is HYDOR, which means a liquid state and is the root of the word hydrogen.

Although he seemed to stress the physical properties of water, Thales said that it was "full of gods." By this he meant that water was animated: the conveyer of the NOUS, the soul.

Following Thales lead philosophy flourished throughout the sixth century B.C. Pythagoras and his followers studied mathematics and music in an attempt to understand the KOSMOS, a word they coined to convey the idea of the "Kinship of the Universe." Heraclitus, another Greek philosopher, claimed that the ultimate reality of the world is a divinely ordered flux, a LOGOS, which he described as a river. He said: "Into the same river we do and do not step." In other words, the idea of the river is always the same idea, but physically it is never the same. The concept 'river' is permanent but the specific river is always changing. You can't step into the same physical river twice.[1]

Today, we will speak of the Hudson River as a metaphor. Naturalist John Burroughs who lived for many years on the banks of the Hudson, wrote in 1880:

> Rivers are as various in their forms as forest trees. The Mississippi is like an oak with enormous branches. . . .The Hudson is like a pine or poplar – mainly trunk. From New York to Albany there is only an inconsiderable limb or two and but few gnarls. . . .There are some crooked places it is true, but on the whole the Hudson presents a fine symmetrical shaft that would be hard to match in any river of the world.[2]

When Henry Hudson's ship the *Half Moon* sailed in 1609 into the river he passed our site here in search of a polar passage to the Oriental Sea. He knew within a few weeks that this was not an Arctic route and sailed back down to return to Amsterdam. Yet, Hudson pondered the meaning ". . .of his Great River of the Mountains whose alluring mysteries he had penetrated."[3]

Today, his river has become a symbol that inspires us in a spiritual sense and challenges us with its physical dimensions: as we continue to ponder the great river outside our window.

NOTES

1. Drew A. Hyland, *The Origins of Philosophy*, New York: G.P. Putnam's Sons, 1973, p.157.

2. Ernest Ingersoll, *Illustrated Guide to the Hudson River and Catskill Mountains*, Astoria, N.Y.: J.C. & A.L. Fawcett, Inc. Publishers, 1910, (reprinted 1989), p.11.

3. W.M. Williamson, *Henry Hudson Discoverer of the Hudson River 1609*, New York: Museum of the City of New York, 1959, p.7.

Tappan Zee

Harlem River Ship Canal

MR. THOMAS BROSNAN

History of Water Pollution in the Hudson River

GOOD MORNING. I'm a longtime resident of Riverdale and coming back to Mount Saint Vincent brings back a lot of memories to me personally. I used to cut through the campus here to go fishing, back when I was about 12 to 15 years old. Not that I caught very much, but it was fun dodging the guards. Then in later years we found other reasons, myself and my friends, to come back to Mount Saint Vincents, for the dances and the mixers, and so forth. Although I never officially attended here, I kind of feel that I did, as I know the campus very well.

My purpose in talking to you today is really to give you a brief history of water pollution in the Lower Hudson River here in New York Harbor, and the water pollution control efforts that have recently paid off and cleaned up much of the problems in the river, although not all of them. What I'm going to do is give you a brief characterization of what the estuary is. I'll try and give you a brief history of the water pollution control efforts that have occurred, and the benefits that we've observed from our monitoring of the river. I'd like to wrap it up with the remaining issues and problems that remain.

For a little over a hundred years, New York Harbor has been subjected to tremendous loading of pollutants from a 16,000-

1

square mile drainage area, and until relatively recently, this load has included the discharge of millions of gallons of raw or untreated sewage. These raw sewage discharges have caused numerous use curtailments throughout the estuary, including closed shell-fishing beds from high pathogen levels, closed bathing beaches from, again, high pathogen levels, and also from floatables, floating out to the beaches. Low dissolved oxygen causes problems for the fish and other organisms living there. Just part of the problem are toxic metals and other organic compounds, pesticides and things like that. They have caused a variety of impacts both to fish that live in the water and also, moving up the food chain, to birds. Ultimately they can cause problems for higher organisms including humans.

Therefore, it is with good reason that water quality planners for much of the century have grappled with the problem of trying to abate the discharge of these millions of gallons of raw sewage from the City and the whole region. We're talking about New Jersey, Westchester, Rockland, the whole area – millions of gallons of raw sewage that have been discharged from the cities and have reached millions of residents.

I would like to give you a brief overview of what an estuary is: An estuary by definition is a place where fresh water and salt water meet. The salinity out here just off Mount Saint Vincent is typically in the summer, five to ten parts per thousand salinity. If you go a few miles upstream, it is about zero parts per thousand, which is freshwater. If you go to just off the Rockaways, off Rockaway Beach, the open ocean is about 32 parts per thousand. What you're looking at out here is about two-thirds saltwater and one-third freshwater from the Hudson River.

The Hudson River is part of the Greater Hudson Raritan estuarine system which includes the Hudson River, Passaic, Hackensack and Raritan Rivers. Out of the 16,000 square miles total coming from New Jersey and New York, about 13,000 square miles are drained by the Hudson River itself. The Hudson dominates the system. Eighty-seven percent of the total flow to the system comes down the Hudson. The summer average is about 15 billion gallons per day of water coming down the Hudson.

Actually, the amount that comes *up* from the ocean drowns that out by many orders of magnitude. Really, the estuary is more dominated by the ocean than it is by the river.

The residence time of the river is about 15 days in the spring or 60 days in the summer. The way to think of that is, when you discharge the pollutants into the river in the spring, it takes about 15 days to flush itself out, with the high river flows coming down and making the flushing rate quicker; in the summer, it will take about 60 days. Typically, water quality problems are worse in the summer – there are higher temperatures, residence times are higher, flushing rates are lower, and more people are out using the water so water quality problems directly impact people. Typically, when we look at worst-case conditions with water, we look at them in the summer.

I'd like to give you a brief history now of water pollution control efforts that have gone on in the region. Waste water collection and sewer construction in the City started in about the year 1696, with much of Lower Manhattan's sewers constructed in the 1800s. The first waste water treatment facility was built in New York City in 1896. It was just a floatable stream facility to protect the beaches at Coney Island. In 1906, the Metropolitan Sewage Commission was formed to study water pollution in New York Harbor. Water pollution was getting to be a very serious problem back in the early part of this century, with fisheries and bathing beaches being closed, and people getting sick from eating contaminated shellfish. Therefore, this Commission was formed.

We have some of the earlier documents from when this Commission did the studies of the harbor. They did extensive water quality studies of the harbor; they looked at fisheries, they looked at the pollutants, and they documented their information very well. These papers are really a pleasure to read if you're interested in history. They put some of us to shame today, as we review the quality of information that they collected. And their conclusions were right on! They knew exactly what needed to be done in order to clean up the harbor. It unfortunately took about 80 years to implement because it was, and is, a massive problem.

Roughly eight million people are living or employed within New York City and twenty million live within 50 miles of the City. When the Metropolitan Sewage Commission started the study in 1906, they reported floating seas of garbage throughout the estuary and increased discharges of raw sewage and industrial effluence. There was also habitat loss on a major scale. The wetlands, which used to dot and cover many areas of the harbor, especially on the Jersey side but also on the New York side were lost, due to dredging and filling. This destruction of wetlands has had at least as much of a detrimental impact on water quality and the habitat of New York Harbor as pollutants have had. While you can abate pollutant loadings, it's very tough to get back habitat once you have destroyed it, although there have been some limited cases of success.

By the 1930s, several fisheries in the region had already been shut down, including smelt, menhaden, sturgeon, hard and soft shell clams. The fantastic oyster fisheries, which was nationally renowned at a minimum and world-renowned in some cases, that existed around Staten Island were closed due to outbreaks of typhoid, resulting from people eating contaminated shellfish. Numerous people died in 1904 in Jamaica Bay, and in 1914 in Raritan Bay from oyster contamination. The oyster fisheries were completely shut down by 1925, and have not reopened to this day.

One thing that the Metropolitan Sewage Commission did was to institute a water quality monitoring program starting in 1909 which, I am happy to say, is still in effect today. It is probably the longest-running water quality monitoring program, certainly in this country. The only longer-running project that I know of is for the Thames River in England, which was started in the late 1800s and called the Harbor Survey Program.

We presently have a long-term data base in our Harbor Survey Program. I'm the manager of it. We have 52 stations where we monitor the river year-round for a variety of water pollutants. We have a good sense of where the rivers have been and where they're going to, and there have been dramatic improvements.

The first modern sewage treatment plants were constructed in the 1930s, including Coney Island, the East River, New Jersey and also the Yonkers treatment plant just north of this campus. They've had a major beneficial impact on the river.

In the 1980s, New York City constructed its final two plants out of 14 planned. Over the years from the '30s up to the '80s, the City constructed a variety of treatment plants all throughout the City. Unfortunately, the Hudson River treatment plants were late in coming. The one on the Hudson River north of 125th Street, called the North River treatment plant, was one of the last to be constructed. When that was completed in the spring of 1986, it abated the discharge of 170 million gallons per day of raw sewage going into the river. Really, that is not too long ago. Up to ten years ago, there were 170 million gallons of raw, untreated sewage going into the Hudson every day, and there were also 40 million gallons going into the Lower East River. A treatment plant was built there in 1988 and now the city has virtually complete capacity to treat all of its huge amount of raw sewage, which is on the order of a billion and a half gallons per day.

With treatment plants coming on line, water quality improvements have been observed. Two water quality indicators which we examine are dissolved oxygen and the levels of coliform bacteria. Dissolved oxygen is critical for virtually every form of life in the water. They need to breathe it for respiration the same as we need to breathe it. There are state standards that require a minimum amount of dissolved oxygen in the water to keep it fit for aquatic life. One of the ways to determine improvements and abatement of sewage is to look at the dissolved oxygen in the water.

Dissolved oxygen was at its worst in the harbor from the 1920s to 1960s, when concentrations were often less than a part per million. Very few organisms can live at a part per million; they either flee, or if they are attached to the bottom, like worms, shellfish, and things like that, they simply die. So, up until about the 1960s, we had chronic problems every summer, with fish kills, or organisms simply having to leave the area with its very low oxygen. When the treatment plants came on line, we steadily could see the dissolved oxygen rising, especially after the

North River treatment plant came on line and the Yonkers treatment plant was upgraded to secondary treatment. Dissolved
oxygen now in the 1990s is routinely above 3 and 4 milligrams
per liter or parts per million of dissolved oxygen, which is really much, much healthier for the fish. Anecdotally I'll give you
some information on how the ecosystem has responded in terms
of the fisheries and other organisms.

Coliform bacteria is the other major indicator we looked at.
Raw, untreated sewage has concentrations of coliform bacteria in
the millions, so therefore if you find high concentrations in your
water, you know you have untreated sewage discharges in your
water. The states set water quality standards for bathing beaches and shellfishing beds based on coliform bacteria. You have to
have low coliform bacteria counts in your water to bathe or fish
for shellfish there. If they're elevated, your beaches are closed.
It's the number one cause for closing shellfish beds in the area.
In the mid-1980s, the coliform concentrations off Manhattan
were evidence of gross pollution: It wouldn't even be safe to
stick your hand in the water, for example, if you had a cut or
anything like that. There was a problem with meeting even secondary contact standards. Again, with construction of the North
River treatment plant, coliform concentrations dropped by
about 70 percent.

We recently have had some more improvements due to abatement of other miscellaneous sources and, believe it or not,
presently for much of the harbor including the Hudson River,
during average conditions swimming standards are being met.
This is an amazing difference from even ten years ago. There are
other miscellaneous improvements that you can point to in the
estuary: one is an increase in striped bass. Although that increase
is mainly due to the absence of pressure to close the fishery due
to toxins and other problems. There have been decreases in lead
and other metals, and decreases in insecticides and PCBs in the
sediments.

There have been increases in wood-boring organisms; these
are organisms called gribbles. There have been a few reports recently in the papers when a pier collapsed down in the lower

East River, which forced the shutdown of the East Side Drive because these wood-boring organisms ate away the highway's wooden piers. Previously we didn't have gribbles and wood-worms because the water was so bad they couldn't live there. As the water quality got better, these things came back. Here was an unforeseen impact, organisms eating the things in the harbor. If you have a pier, or (God forbid!) a wooden boat in the harbor, you know you have a major problem. It just goes to show you that no good deed goes unpunished because this is causing millions of dollars of damage to piers. We've had meetings with some of the harbor timber officials where they aired the problem and suggested alternate solutions. For example, they stated that, while it's nice to have the water clean, maybe you could ratchet back a little bit, i.e. pollute more and get rid of the gribbles – but of course we're not going to do that.

There's also the return of the peregrine falcons and ospreys. The peregrines are back probably due to breeding improvements largely due to abatement or product bans, of insecticides and things like that. Ospreys have also returned to places like Jamaica Bay. Wading-birds have also come back in a big way throughout the Arthur Kill area and in the Upper East River. We've opened 67,000 acres of shellfish beds in the Lower Harbor since 1985, and we've opened a few beaches since 1988. Seagate Beach on Coney Island is open for the first time in 40 years, and South Midland Beach on Staten Island opened for the first time in 25 years, in 1992.

There are a few remaining water problems – we've come a long way but certain impairments do remain. Number one for many people is fish consumption advisories. Danger still exists due to PCB contamination of the sediments in the Hudson River, which is a long-term problem. This contamination is largely due to discharges from the General Electric Company way upstream, above Albany, back in 1976, I believe, when the entire river was contaminated. We're still living with this 20 years later. We still have fish consumption advisories: where it used to indicate you should eat other fish, now they say you can eat one Hudson River fish per month, or something like that. The advisory still exists primarily due to PCB contamination. Some shellfish beds are still closed due to PCB contamination. Other shellfish beds are still closed due to pathogens and maybe toxins.

Also, you have a very difficult time now disposing of dredged material. This has been highlighted in the newspapers recently when an article stated that we might not be able to go to the Statue of Liberty soon because the sediments which accumulate naturally in the estuary every year are contaminated with various toxins. The problem is once the sediments are dredged, what do you do with them? It's now a big problem. In the past we were able to dump the sediment with the toxins out in the ocean. There's been a lot of controversy with that. But if you cannot dredge up the sediments the commercial port could be closed. The estuary is a natural sediment trap. Everything tends to settle here. Naturally, if you want to keep your port open for commerce, you have to dredge. The big problem now is, what do you do with the material?

Finally, there are episodic beach closures, primarily due to pathogens, sometimes floatables, although I'm happy to say that that is more and more becoming a thing of the past. In New York City, however, there haven't been any beach closings due to floatables since 1989. I think we've made real progress there.

In conclusion, untreated sewage discharges have declined from about a billion gallons a day in the 1930s to less than a million gallons per day today. Dissolved oxygen has increased significantly, coliform bacteria has decreased significantly, and there have been demonstrable improvements in the environment other than those. Although we have come a long way, there are still remaining impairments to be dealt with.

Ice Harvesting

9

The River Project Pier

10

The River Environment

I'M VERY pleased to be up here today and it's great to have an excuse to come up river. We came up along the river all the way from Manhattan to a few blocks from here and enjoyed seeing your beautiful trees, grass, and all those other things we don't have – peace and quiet. I, however, am a diehard, chauvinistic Manhattanite, a real City lover, and I've lived in Manhattan all my adult life. I fell in love with it when I first saw it at 10 years of age, when my mother brought me to town. Right away I said to myself, this is where I want to live – I felt so comfortable there, and I still do.

What I want to talk to you about today is the waters of our world, but first, I'd like to tell you a little bit about myself, something I don't think I've ever done in front of a microphone before. This concept of applied philosophy is a new one to me. When I saw that this was The Institute for Applied Philosophy, I thought, "Oh, gee! Applied Philosophy!" Now I'm starting today to think that anything we do with The River Project is explainable in applied philosophy, and I feel I can fit right in and review for you what the speakers ahead of me have said.

My life story starts at about age 30. Before that, it was a sort of permanent vacation. At the age of 30, by accident, someone took me snorkeling and scuba diving, and I just fell in love with what I saw in the water and I said, "Now I know what I want to do with my life." I went back to school, which I had dropped out of at quite an early age, got my Bachelor of Science degree from Columbia in molecular biology, and went on to do marine science at the Marine Science Center at the State University of New York (SUNY). I already knew exactly what I wanted to study and exactly what I wanted to do.

The reason I went back to school was that I had to in order to do the things I wanted. I had inherited some money from my grandmother which I blew by going around the world for two years, and was able to go scuba diving in what are still some of the most phenomenal spots on the planet – off the Solomon Islands, the Great Barrier Reef in Australia, many places in the Caribbean. I think I've seen some of the most beautiful sights, including some spots where nobody had ever been underwater before, certainly off the Solomons, where a friend had a research vessel. No one had ever fished it, no one had ever been there, and it's a very, very rich underwater habitat.

I was doing underwater photography for many years and I realized that, in the evening, when it came time to socialize, I would rather sit with the scientists than with the photographers. I wasn't so interested in the F stop, but I was very interested in what fish was doing what to whom, and how things were working with what we had seen during the day. Anyhow, this is me. I live in Manhattan. I've lived there right on the Hudson River, looking right out on the river from closer than we are here. You can see it in this painting – to the right of the Statue of Liberty, there's a building there which is outlined in red. That's Pier A, [See painting page x] the southern tip of the west-side waterfront in Manhattan. Just behind that building is what was originally my apartment house. Now across the street is the site of The River Project.

I had a little diving accident at one point and that was the end of career one. When I had to come home and rehabilitate myself and look out the window on the river, the same thing happened to me that happened to President Stuart: I became completely enthralled with the river. I'm looking out every day and wondering what's in there – I'm used to snorkeling and being able to see what's on the bottom. We used to take a little grid down, and go to the same spot every day and record every fish. If coral is unhealthy, you'd see it. In the Hudson River, however, there is no visibility to speak of. Anything we know of it, is through secondary information of some kind; some way of measuring something that leads you to conclude that something is happening, but you really cannot see most of it.

I brought prior experience with me when I was looking out on the river and wondering, "What's in there? – I wonder if I could catch some fish in there?" Finally, I got permission. Living across the street from the old West Side Highway – some of you may know it because it's an extremely political site on the river called the Westway Corridor. It's a four mile stretch and is the largest parcel of real estate in the country, held as one parcel, on the waterfront, that will ever be developed as one development. In this case, it will be mostly a park. Some areas of it have been sold out in the plan, to support the park, so that it won't need outside money from other agencies. It will be a self-sustaining park, a self-funded park.

There has been about fifteen to twenty years of litigation that has resulted in everything being so tied up that nobody can do anything on any of those piers along the west side of Manhattan: add that to the ice damage over the years and the problems with nobody really being authorized to go in and repair anything, and the conditions that Tom described to you with the gribbles eating away at the piers and pylons. So the piers are really falling into the river while all kinds of arguments and litigation have gone on about what should happen there. In a way, that has been a big boon to the living resources because the habitat amongst what we call the inter-pier, under-pier area has been virtually undisturbed for 56 years and maybe before that. For example there's an awful lot of stuff in there, right behind Pier A.

We know from other studies that behind the Statue of Liberty, there are at least 127 species of fish in the water, and, in fact, the harbor still maintains all the original spawning stock that were here when Henry Hudson arrived. This is a miracle in itself, because in every other estuary on the east coast, the ecosystem and the natural living resources of the estuaries have pretty much collapsed. The only reason the Hudson has escaped that kind of collapse is not because we managed our resources any better or were any kinder to the environment, but because of the accident of having alkaline rock as geological formations that washed into the river, which buffers acid rain. Acid rain was the final straw that broke the camel's back in other estuaries.

After all the pollutant loading that Tom Brosnan described to you, add on the effects of acid rain which I think may have abated somewhat as well in the last several years but was certainly strong earlier. Some of the most valuable living treasures and legacies that belong to us are packed here, so we should guard them. In this politically enlightened era – most people recognize that – and as Tom says, the government, the City government mostly, but now State government and Federal government, have gone a long way with sewage treatment plants and other upgrades to clean up the water. I am, in fact, one of the few people who does swim in the river. Tom told you that some of those areas are safe to use as beach areas or for fishing but we should be careful how we use them even now. The water quality is consistent with swimming but there are, of course, areas not designated as swimming areas where we swim anyway between the pier heads off Lower Manhattan. We do this sagaciously while exercising applied philosophy.

There is a clause we quote you now, chapter and verse, from the EPA Clean Water Act which says "The Federal Government must maintain water quality standards in the area consistent with current usage." Tom can probably sort me out on this. How naive I was when we first started! I thought, "OK, great, let's all jump in the river and start swimming, then the Feds will have to clean up the river consistent with swimming." This was probably the most constructive thing we could do. Today, there's a group of us who do swim in the river. It's getting some attention and it's very, very lovely to do on a day when you don't feel a lot of floatables around – at the right time of the tide and on the right day. Anyhow, this is how The River Project itself was started.

I got a permit from the City to go over to the pier and deploy some instruments and start fishing. Then all my old pals from marine science came on board to help. We went exploring the boats and boat owners. I put something off the pier. Then the questions arose – can we do this afloat – or maybe we've got to incorporate – maybe we've got to get insurance – maybe we've got to get a permit from the City. Bit by bit over the last 10 years we've had to become quite civilized in that way, and from a couple of raving radicals just mucking around in the water, we've become a quite civilized group with all the right papers and pantyhose and things like that. So I'm terror-proof about the forms and proofs we're all going to need if somebody strong is not salaried. We have now gotten permission to occupy the sheds and the pier, one of these piers that are falling down, and as a tribute to Tom's work on the river, it was just condemned again last week for the third time. Luckily we've been saved by some State and City money going toward making the repairs so that we're able to continue our summer program.

The River Project at this point includes research, education and wetland restoration or attempts at habitat restoration. I call it wetlands, but it is some sort of attempt at applying philosophies of restoring habitat in an urban area. In other words, we're saying, just because we live in the City, how come we can't have the wading-birds and the butterflies and the beautiful coastal shrubs and plants that everybody else along the river has? Well, there's really no reason other than political why we too can't have that as part of our waterfront park. So a bunch of us gave up some time, started sitting around with each other, and drew up a plan that really had no link with reality. We said, "Let's just put down here what we would really want if it were a dream come true." We said, "That's the new park we want landscaped in our way instead of building this immense, heavily financed, vertical bulkhead such as we built all around the City, which has eradicated the most productive beds of the harbor estuary in the intertidal flows." We said, "Can we maybe do something to restore some of the cement vertical bulkheads like this?" The tide goes up and down, we have a five foot tidal reach.

But now there is a habitat. If there's a float on a beach or where the tide goes up and down, you have an area that is alternately submerged and exposed. That's one of the two things that characterizes an estuary – that it becomes very, very rich, probably more rich in species diversity and the number of organisms than most of the rain forests of the world. Yet is part of the engineering thinking of the last century, which I think of as a sort of male-dominated idea of control, like, "We'll wall up the river, we'll control it, we'll dominate it, we can know everything that happens on it, it'll be predictable, we'll know." We're saying, what about a soft green edge, something more gentle and something that could sustain life.

We put down some beautiful, dreamlike visions of this sort of thing and, amazingly enough, there was a lot of support for it in New York City. And people like Mr. Woods, who is going to talk to you in a little while, saying a kind word about us was enough for us to put down roots there. We're working very hard there now on these issues, trying to keep our connection to the philosophical ideas that have lifted this stuff up. I think of morals and the sea. "Moral" derives from the same word as mother, the sea is our mother, and I certainly felt that all my life. At the age of six, my Mom took me to the ocean. I remember getting rolled over by a big wave and just being in love with the water ever since. As a water creature, we do come from the mud, and we do come from the water.

If any of you are in the City, please come and visit. The River Project is open at Pier 26 Saturday and Sunday, 11:00 to 4:00, or any other time by appointment. We have a 2,000 gallon aquarium system there, with river water running right through it, with animals that we catch off the pier. They're basically in the same environment that they were caught in, so they're very, very healthy and very interesting. It's amazing how little is known about these animals in the fish community yet we find these things all the time. I've caught three species of fish that have never been caught before in the river, which is amazing because I'm using a six-dollar Killy trap like a child would use, and we have no funding for it at all.

Anyway, there is hope down in our area, and we're very much believers in a beautiful new park on the West Side waterfront. A lot of the ideas we get of what our waterfront should look like come from up here on your waterfront, and I'm very very pleased that I've been invited to speak and hear all the other speakers.

Storm King

19

Staten Island Ferry

DR. PETER DERRICK

Crossing the Hudson

HAVING HEARD the previous two speakers, with their emphasis on environmental issues, I have been thinking about why I was asked to come and talk about the Hudson River. All I know about the Hudson River is from crossing it. I go across the river when I go to New Jersey or if I take the Thruway to go upstate. I'm not a naturalist and I don't have any training in environmental science. I am, rather, a transportation planner. I think about the Hudson River from another point of view, not so much as a natural resource but as a barrier to the movement of people and goods in the metropolitan area. That's what I'm going to talk about today. I'm going to provide a very brief overview of efforts that have been made to overcome the Hudson River barrier as a crossing for people and freight. Then I'm going to talk a little about what's happening today both with respect to ferries as well as in the way of some interesting plans to improve rail service across the Hudson River.

Mr. Brosnan pointed out at the end of his talk that we have a problem with the fact that concern for the environment of the river has stopped the dredging of the river, and that this may have a long-term effect on the economic prosperity of the region. This is because if the New York/New Jersey metropolitan area ceases to function as a port, or is greatly diminished as a port, this will result in a loss of jobs and loss of commerce. I think we're facing a similar problem with respect to transportation crossings of the river. If we cannot deal adequately with the problems people have in crossing the river, this may have a detrimental effect on the region's economy.

Many people don't understand that the Hudson River has been a barrier for centuries. As I was thinking about what I was going to say at this conference, I happened to be reading a book called *The Alienist* by Caleb Carr. It's a novel set in New York City in the 1890s when Theodore Roosevelt was Police Commissioner. In one of the episodes in the book, the heroes of the book, who live in Greenwich Village, take their hansom cab up to Grand Central Terminal. Then they take a train from Grand Central Terminal to Washington. I'd like to read you that part: "Sara accompanied us into Grand Central when we arrived, and then to the platform where the Washington train stood in steaming readiness ... the loud whistle on the train's engine screamed and the conductor's smaller pipe began to wail, signalling us to get on board." Then the train pulls out of Grand Central, and the writer says, "I was unconscious for over two hours, and woke to see rich green New Jersey pastures shooting by the window."

Well, there's something wrong with this-- getting on a train in 1895 at Grand Central and going directly to Washington. The first thing is, you have never been able to get on a train at Grand Central and go directly to Washington. This was certainly true in the 1890s, because there were no rail or highway crossings of the Hudson River. Moreover, even after a rail tunnel for intercity trains was built between New Jersey and New York in the first decade of this century it went to Pennsylvania Station, not Grand Central Terminal.

Until the turn of this century, the way you got to Washington from Manhattan was you first took a ferry boat to New Jersey. The railroads terminated there because it was very costly to build tunnels under the Hudson, and very difficult to do from an engineering point of view. In New Jersey, you boarded a train to Washington. From 1910, when the Pennsylvania Railroad opened service under the Hudson to Penn Station, until the present day, if you wanted to go to Washington directly from New York, you took a train from Penn.

This raises a question: What was the matter with ferry boats? Why, if it was so costly and difficult to build a rail tunnel under the Hudson, couldn't people keep on using ferries? The answer to this has to do with the capacity of ferries and with the long travel times involved in using them, as opposed to direct service by rail between New York and New Jersey.

New York was a very rapidly growing city in 1900, with large increases occurring each year in the number of people traveling to and from Manhattan. People who were coming to the city from west of the Hudson River, whether they were living there and commuting to work every day, or whether they were taking long intercity trips from places like Washington or Atlanta, had several problems in crossing the Hudson River. The first was that ferries did not have the capacity to carry large numbers of people in a short period of time. That is to say, the number of people a ferry boat could carry was small compared to a railroad train. The sheer volumes of customers at ferry terminals cried out for relief of congestion. Moreover, this problem was expected to get worse as the number of trips to the city increased. Secondly, the longer trip travel times in using ferries and the inconvenience of making many transfers was something that bothered a lot of people. Most people will avoid transfers and try to reduce their travel times whenever possible.

As a result of these factors, it seemed clear to railroad companies and private investors that people would be willing to pay for faster and more convenient transportation across the Hudson, and that large profits could be made by providing such service. Thus, railroad executives, engineers and planners looked to see what they could do about these shortcomings. In terms of rail crossings, the end result was the construction between 1900 and 1910 of the only rail tunnels under the Hudson River that have ever built.

The first system to be built was what we now call "the PATH System" – the Port Authority Trans-Hudson System – that used to be the lines of the Hudson and Manhattan Railroad Company. PATH has a terminal in Hoboken; and it has two other stops in Jersey City close to the Hudson River, one at Exchange Place, the other at Pavonia. There are two lines under the Hudson, one that goes to the Wall Street area and another that enters New York in Greenwich Village and then passes under Sixth Avenue to 33rd Street. One of the reasons for the construction of the Hudson and Manhattan System was to connect the rail terminals on the Jersey waterfront to Manhattan. People could get off at those terminals and get on what was essentially a subway line, and come into the Wall Street area, or, on the other line, go into Midtown. The Hudson and Manhattan System also had other stops in Jersey City and other places that served local residents of these areas. Its ridership was always a combination of commuters transferring from commuter rail lines to complete the trip to Manhattan as well as customers using the line to get from local residential areas to New York.

Thoughts of creating such a system had started in the 1870s but there were technical and financial problems. Construction was started on a tunnel in the 1870s but there were blowouts and other problems. Construction workers who were building it actually got sucked into the Hudson River. The result was that construction was halted. It was only at the turn of the century that the work was picked up again, in part because tunnelling methods had improved.

The second thing that happened between the 1870s and the turn of the century was the whole development of something called "electric traction," that is to say, powering trains by electricity by third rail. The Hudson and Manhattan System was an electric subway. It opened in 1908 and was the first high capacity crossing of the Hudson River directly to the city. (In 1962 the lines of the bankrupt Hudson and Manhattan Railroad Company were taken over by The Port of New York Authority – now the Port Authority of New York and New Jersey – and service has since been provided by a PA subsidiary, the Port Authority Trans-Hudson Corporation, or PATH. Since the 1960s all public transit in the New York metropolitan area has been subsidized by the government and is not expected to make a profit.)

The other rail crossing was accomplished by the great competitor to the New York Central (which came into Grand Central Terminal), the Pennsylvania Railroad, which up until 1910 had terminated rail passenger service at the Jersey waterfront. The railroad was having problems competing with the New York Central, especially for trips from the Midwest to New York City. They saw tremendous market opportunities in providing direct service to Manhattan from the South and the Midwest. As a result, the Pennsylvania developed a major plan for rail improvements throughout the New York area, which included a two-track line under the Hudson to the vast new terminal, Pennsylvania Station, between Seventh and Eighth Avenues from 31st to 33rd Streets.

There was a long political battle over this. I'm not going to go into the details, but the final outcome was the opening of this first, and only, direct intercity rail line from New Jersey to New York in 1910. The two-track line from New Jersey proceeds into Penn Station, which has 21 tracks. From Penn Station the line continues across Manhattan and under the East River to Queens, via four tracks. (The tracks under the Hudson are now used by AMTRAK and by the State of New Jersey's transit agency, New Jersey Transit. The tracks under the East River are now used by MTA Long Island Rail Road, which was a subsidiary of the Pennsylvania Railroad until it was purchased by New York State in 1965 via the predecessor agency of the Metropolitan Transportation Authority; by New Jersey Transit to get to its storage yards in Queens; and by AMTRAK for service to New England and Canada via the Hell Gate Bridge and The Bronx. There is also a line that proceeds from Penn Station north along the West Side of Manhattan, across the Spuyten Duyvil Bridge into The Bronx and on to upstate New York. AMTRAK provides passenger service on this line.)

The Pennsylvania Railroad system represented a major overcoming of the Hudson barrier, but it had one major limitation. The rail tunnel under the Hudson River was built only for passengers because it was decided to power the trains coming in there with electric traction. Freight trains powered by coal-fired steam locomotives, and later by diesel fuel, could not be run through the tunnel because of ventilation problems. Therefore the problem of rail freight remained. Freight railroads had to terminate west of the Hudson and the goods had to be ferried across to Manhattan. Thus, even though the passenger problem was temporarily alleviated by 1910, the freight problem continued.

From 1910 until today no new rail lines have been built across the Hudson. Meanwhile, on the New York side of the river, several lines of the New York subway were built under and over the East River. Between 1910 and 1933, nine subway crossings of the East River were placed in operation. The result was a boom in population in the "subway suburbs" of Brooklyn and Queens between 1910 and 1950. Further rail crossings of the Hudson, in contrast, were stymied by a lack of political will on both sides of the river.

This lack of political will is represented by what happened to the Port Authority with respect to the building of a freight rail connection from New Jersey to New York. Most people don't realize that the Port Authority of New York and New Jersey was created in the early 1920s primarily to build a union freight tunnel under the harbor, from New Jersey to Brooklyn, so that you would have direct rail freight access to Brooklyn and Queens, and then, through these areas, to have better freight access to Manhattan. This has never happened.

After the Port Authority was frustrated by its inability to get the railroads together and to figure out how to pay for a freight tunnel, the agency concentrated on a new moneymaker, the automobile. From the late 1920s on, the Port Authority moved to fulfill the desire of people to use their private automobiles to go places in the region. Just as we had the need for rail tunnels up to 1910, now there was a perceived need for vehicular tunnels, that is to say, tunnels that could carry cars and trucks. The need was not pressing until the 1920s.

What the Port Authority did was to get into the bridge and tunnel business. They took over the Holland Tunnel (opened

1927), which was the first vehicular tunnel to come from Jersey City to Lower Manhattan. They constructed the Lincoln Tunnel (opened 1937) and they built the George Washington Bridge (opened 1931). These are the Hudson River crossings that have been built between Manhattan and New Jersey since 1910. (The only other new crossing of the Hudson in the metropolitan area that has been built since the 1930s is the Thruway's Tappan Zee Bridge that opened in the early 1950s. In addition, a second level was added to the George Washington Bridge.)

The inability to build new transportation lines has had an impact on real estate values. Today, one of the reasons that you can buy a cheaper house, of the same quality, in New Jersey than in New York is that you cannot commute from New Jersey to Manhattan easily. From the 1950s on, as families looked for reasonable houses to buy in the suburbs and saw that the prices of homes in Westchester and Nassau counties were so high that they couldn't possibly afford to buy one, many decided to cross the Hudson to New Jersey. The average home price is cheaper in Bergen and Rockland counties, to give two examples, than it is east of the Hudson, again for a house of equal quality.

From the 1950s on, there was this growing increase in the number of people living in New Jersey and working in New York City or in other areas this side of the river. Yet there has been no increase in the capacity of the Hudson River crossings from New Jersey, except for the second deck of the George Washington Bridge. Meanwhile, as more people decided to live west of the Hudson and work east of the Hudson traffic naturally has continued to increase. Anybody who tries to cross the George Washington Bridge during the rush hour finds that you have a normal wait time during the rush hour of 20 to 40 minutes just to pay a toll, a four-dollar toll, to get into New York City. The same thing is true of the Lincoln Tunnel and the Holland Tunnel.

These are the types of problems that transportation planners focus on. Commuters to Manhattan from New Jersey have relatively long travel times due to severe congestion on the Hudson River vehicular crossings and the inconvenient transit connections from many areas. As a result, you have the planners saying,

"We have this capacity problem, we've got to fix it."

Trying to deal with the current problems in crossing the Hudson River, we have seen ferries make a comeback during the past ten years. Except for the Staten Island ferry, by the 1970s public ferries in New York Harbor had gone out of business, defeated in part by the very success of the rail and highway crossings of the Hudson and East rivers.

In recent years, however, the Port Authority has supported the opening of a ferry from Hoboken to Lower Manhattan, aimed at relieving PATH. In addition, a private company, New York Waterways, operates ferries from New Jersey to Midtown and to Lower Manhattan. Numerous other ferry services have also opened recently or are on the drawing boards. The drawback with ferries, however, goes back to the late nineteenth century: A ferry cannot carry very many people.

The new ferry service from Hoboken to Lower Manhattan carries only a few thousand people a day. During the next two decades, however, the number of people living in New Jersey and working in Manhattan is expected to increase by tens of thousands, putting further pressure on the limited capacity of existing rail and highway crossings of the Hudson. The only feasible high capacity solution is a new rail line. With this in mind, the Port Authority, in a joint effort with the Metropolitan Transportation Authority (MTA) and New Jersey Transit, is examining whether new rail lines across the Hudson should be built. This effort is called the Access to the Region's Core (ARC) Study.

There are a number of ways to cross the Hudson River. One undertaking might be to come from the Meadowlands area with a new rail tunnel either to Penn Station, or to Midtown Manhattan in the 40s, for example across 49th Street. This line would connect with existing commuter rail service West of the Hudson, now provided by New Jersey Transit. The ARC study has already determined that a new commuter rail line from New Jersey to Manhattan with direct service to the East Side, where tens of thousands of west of Hudson residents work, would carry large numbers of passengers each day. Such a line could first enter Manhattan in the Penn Station area and then proceed under Manhattan to the lower level of Grand Central Terminal in the heart of the East Side. [See page 31 for a map of this proposal.] Subway crossings of the Hudson are also possible.

Another approach might be to come from Rockland County to tie in with MTA Metro-North Railroad's Hudson Line on the east shore of the Hudson that proceeds into Grand Central Terminal. This potential crossing, however, already seems to have been defeated. The idea of crossing the river in the Rockland-Westchester area was being explored by MTA Metro-North Railroad, but it got caught up in the same problem Mr. Brosnan talked about. A Hudson crossing would have had to come through the Palisades to proceed under the river to the Hudson Line, and for good, logical reasons, the residents living in the area were very upset at the threat of disturbing their environment. In the end, the study was shelved.

That gets us back to where I want to finish. You have a situation where there is another major study, ARC, being done to look at building new rail crossings of the Hudson River. It's clear that there is no will, and there should be no will, to build any new highways across the Hudson via bridges or tunnels. The New York metropolitan area is in violation of the Clean Air Act, and there are all sorts of environmental problems that would result from adding highway capacity, so nobody wants to do that and nobody is talking about doing that.

As part of ARC, professional transportation planners, after holding numerous public meetings and having done extensive analysis, have produced information on several options to build new rail tunnels under the Hudson River. Many of these alternatives would increase the speed of service to and from New Jersey and Orange and Rockland counties and Manhattan. Right now, to provide an example, if you live in Orange County, it takes you almost an hour and a half to travel to Manhattan. If you had direct rail service to the East Side, the travel time each way would be reduced by 20 or 30 minutes. That's the type of thing that's being looked at.

As of yet, however, the ARC proposals have received very little political support. Transportation planners deal with issues such as travel time and the capacity of the transit system. But, in the end, in order to proceed with building anything, the debate gets into this "philosophy thing," we've talked about previously. At the turn of the century, there were corporate types leading the major railroad companies whose main aim was to make sure that new transportation lines were actually built, rather than just being talked about. If, in terms of Gilbert & Sullivan, there was the very model of a modern major general, the typical railroad man was the very model of the corporate type. These men pushed through the building of the last rail line that was built from New Jersey to New York – the Pennsylvania Railroad crossing into Penn Station and on to Long Island and even to New England. Since then nothing has happened. The public officials responsible for transit across the Hudson since the 1960s have done much to improve existing transit service but have not been able to build any new lines (There was a very model of a modern major public official, who did build a lot of things, but Robert Moses was concerned only with highways and bridges East of the Hudson and had no use for transit proposals!)

Right now what you've got is a situation where the three major transit agencies in the region, New Jersey Transit, the MTA, and the Port Authority, have supported a study that has produced detailed information on the costs and benefits of a number of alternatives, with one of the more promising options being the line crossing the Hudson into the Penn Station area and then proceeding on to Grand Central Terminal. But what has to be dealt with, and rightly so, is: What do the people really want? It's a complicated thing because people differ and that gets us back to the philosophy: What do the people really think they need and what are they willing to pay for? And how do we make these choices? A good intellectual case can be made to dig new rail tunnels under the Hudson River. Although there might be some small disturbance of the environment, new rail service would allow more convenient trips into Manhattan, and would bolster the attraction of Manhattan as a world center of business. Is that a good thing or is that a bad thing? That, again, has to do with the perspective people have: What is their main concern?

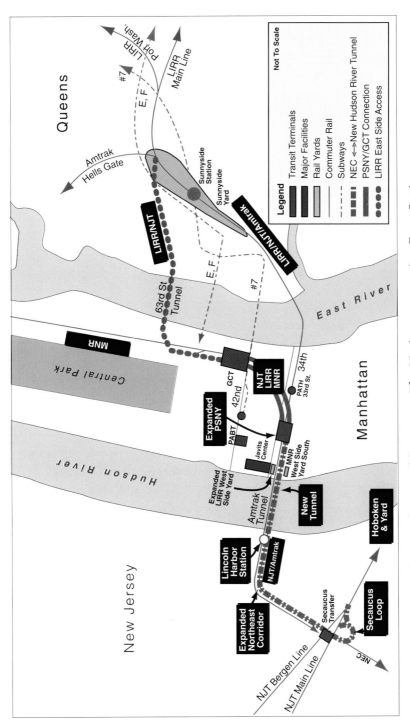

Proposed new rail line across The Hudson, connecting Penn Station,
Grand Central Terminal and the 63rd Street Tunnel.
Courtesy of Access to the Region's Core (ARC) Study.

The Access to the Region's Core Study has had many meetings about various rail alternatives with representatives of the business community in the region. There's interest there because they see it as something that will create jobs and economic development and build up New York City and its suburbs as an urban region that continues to be the rival of other "World Cities" such as Tokyo, London and Paris. In this regard, Tokyo and Paris, and other major business centers such as Seoul and Singapore, have built hundreds of miles of new rail lines since the 1950s, and many of these urban regions are now building even more lines. Unlike these other cities, however, it's questionable whether we have the political will to expand the rail system anywhere in the region to meet the transportation needs of the 21st century.

For more than a half a century, the physical barrier of the Hudson River has been a growing regional problem, in part because the Hudson River also delineates a major political barrier, as it is the borderline between the two states of New York and New Jersey. Although the Port Authority and other agencies have assessed ways of alleviating the physical barrier, reaching a consensus on a new Hudson crossing also will require that the political barrier between the two states (as well as that between New York City and New Jersey!) be crossed. Making this political crossing can only happen if narrower concerns are put aside in favor of taking a longer term perspective. How the region faces this challenge will have a lot to do with how its people and its political leaders think about and frame such major issues. In the end, it will depend, in short, on their underlying philosophies of the kind of place they want the region to be in the coming millennium.

Albany

33

William Underhill Brickyard

DR. ALLAN S. GILBERT

Archaeology in the Hudson Valley:
Preserving an Old Source of New History

I AM pleased to be able to speak to you today about the Hudson River. I am an archaeologist by training, and in practice both an excavator of historic sites and a specialist in the analysis of archaeological materials, but only fairly recently have I begun to pursue research in local archaeology. My interest has grown over the years for reasons beyond the inherent fascination of the historical problems. Throughout America in general, but especially here in New York, the vestiges of the past are in desperate need of advocate voices calling for their protection. As land use has intensified, threatening ever greater numbers of archaeological sites with destruction, communities have found themselves weighing the importance of development against that of preservation. Underlying such conflicts is the question of archaeology's value. Does it truly add to the flavor of history, or does it merely garnish the plate of documentary evidence?

The Hudson River makes a poignant case. Immortalized in travel accounts, reminiscences, history, art, and fiction, it has become one of America's most written-about waterways. But even this vast literature reveals only part of its story. Much of the past still lies beneath the soil, concealed within the buried remains of old campsites, houses, farms, forts, and other marks of a human presence now lost to time. Exposing these remnants and rescuing the information they conceal has without question contributed important new details to the historical record.

The oldest events in the Hudson Valley were never witnessed by humans. Long before the arrival of people in North America, slow transformations in the land merged mountain streams into a river and determined its course to the sea. These changes can still be deciphered by geologists and paleontologists from the physical evidence of rocks and fossils. Archaeology concerns itself with a human time scale that begins at least 10,000 years ago in the Hudson Valley. The prehistoric Native Americans who exploited the natural resources over those ten millennia left no narratives about their life on the river, so only excavation of their ancient sites sheds light on their ways. The arrival of Europeans in the early 1600s finally ushered in the historic period, spawning the chronicles of exploration that give historians their first glimpses of Hudson Valley culture. Looking back over the documentation, however, one can appreciate its unevenness. In places, it is thorough, in others, sketchy or non-existent. Even the later industrial centuries did not leave us with sufficiently detailed depictions of all the events and personalities that shaped the times, and about which we might wish to be better informed. Once more, archaeology provides a means of access to new data.

If the Hudson Valley possessed no vestiges of the past, or if all relics had been obliterated by the march of progress, then one might sadly claim that the written record held the final word, and that only the most recent veneer of human experience was knowable to any great extent. But the Hudson is not bereft of remains. On the contrary, it is quite rich in information yet to be learned.

PRESERVING THE PAST

Though archaeology surely connects us with the past, the present is more intimately involved than many recognize. The present is a critical ingredient in the creation of archaeological knowledge because what we do now profoundly influences the clarity of the evidence. Archaeologists are trained to read the record of the past in the objects and materials left behind, but their ability to discern patterns and draw conclusions depends upon finding remains in a state of good preservation. Disturbances to a site disrupt the arrangement of its contents, separating artifacts that might originally have been closely associated, and destroying or removing pieces of the puzzle. Since archaeologists must read the buried record by digging, their own act of exploration represents a disturbance. They must, therefore, register the information correctly the first time through careful documentation, appropriate curation of finds, and competent analysis, interpretation, and publication. Only high standards of scientific inquiry insure the survival of the physical evidence after the site is no more. There is no second chance.

Unfortunately, the untrained public is not usually as meticulous in its dealings with archaeological deposits. Unless they learn and use proper procedures, work with care, record their efforts, and disseminate their results, those who dig in search of artifacts for personal collections or for profit inflict their own form of permanent devastation upon sites and the information contained within them. Land developers who proceed without the contracted services of archaeologists to find and save the buried evidence prior to its demise also render the past more inaccessible by selectively eliminating clues. Ultimately, history is diminished – or lost a second time – when archaeological research is compromised by site destruction.

The remains of the past that lie within the Hudson Valley – or anywhere else – are precious resources that require conservation efforts commensurate with other environmental concerns. Federal, state, and local regulations enacted since the 1960s have addressed many preservation issues, including the establishment of measures to protect or salvage archaeological remains in harm's way. Thus, the law provides in many cases for recognition of the significance of archaeological sites, and mandates that a means of studying them be devised before a new highway, housing development, or sewer line is built over or through them. Following the letter of the law and protecting or mitigating the destruction of cultural resources takes time and costs money, however. Government or business interests sometimes fail to implement even legally mandated procedures either because of the greater costs, the increased bureaucratic complexity, or simply an insensitivity to the preservation ethic that inspired the laws. Furthermore, government and concerned organizations have not achieved a uniformly high success rate in controlling illicit digging by individuals on public lands despite increased penalties.

There is still insufficient awareness of the value of archaeology, for although few would deny that knowing about the past enhances our lives, many appear unmoved by the loss or abuse of the primary evidence. As a possible cure for this paradox, one might prescribe several doses of applied philosophy. The Institute that welcomes us here clearly advocates by its own name that the philosophical underpinnings of Western Civilization are still relevant to daily life. If, as its etymology proclaims, philosophy is "respect for knowledge," then ignoring or destroying the knowledge as yet undiscovered within archaeological sites hardly emulates the ideals upon which our intellectual foundations are based.

THREE ARCHAEOLOGICAL TOURS THROUGH TIME

The most compelling reasons for protecting archaeological resources from unnecessary destruction are the examples of new knowledge that have grown out of successful archaeological studies. I would therefore like to take you on three short tours into separate eras within the Hudson Valley in order to illustrate how excavation, or analysis of archaeological materials, has offered a unique perspective on the place of the river in the flow of human adaptation.[1]

1. Native American Occupation in the Hudson Valley

Our first excursion explores some of the archaeological remains of ancient Native Americans. The original inhabitants of the Western Hemisphere have left no other form of direct historical evidence, and they have known and exploited the land far longer than any other immigrant population.

Some of the earliest evidence of human occupation in the eastern United States comes from the Hudson Valley.[2] The artifacts recovered are comparable to those of the far western Paleo-Indian cultures known from places such as Clovis and Folsom, New Mexico, and dated between 10,000 and 9000 B.C. Two radiocarbon dates averaging 8700 B.C. from a Paleo-Indian occupation at the Shawnee-Minisink site[3] on the Delaware River near Stroudsburg, Pennsylvania, make it reasonably certain that by at least 10,000 years ago, the Hudson River was home to some of the last Ice Age hunter-gatherers. (One radiocarbon date from Dutchess Quarry Cave in Orange County suggests that prehistoric occupation in the Hudson drainage may have been as early as 10,580 B.C.[4] Because the caribou bone on which the date was based is not universally accepted as being equivalent in time with the human artifacts, this date remains controversial.)

About 7000 years earlier, areas north of New York City had begun to re-emerge from under the huge retreating continental ice sheet. The Hudson trough was flooded with glacial meltwater impounded by the terminal moraine that had formed across what is now Long Island and Staten Island. Rupture of this dam prior to 10,000 B.C. and outflow through the breach at the harbor narrows must have drained the lake in spectacular fashion. Sea level rose in step with the melting ice, and once again the lower Hudson Valley was filled, this time with sea water that established the estuary and introduced tidal conditions far upriver.

Current evidence suggests that the earliest aboriginal groups entered the Hudson Valley at a time of substantial climatic and biotic as well as geographic change. Recovery of ancient pollen indicates that by 8000 B.C., the ecosystem was in transition from an open forest of pine, spruce, and birch to one with increasing numbers of oak and hemlock. Hickory eventually became the principal accompaniment to the oaks, and then the association expanded to include other broad-leaved deciduous species that remain common today.[5]

Many large animals are known to have inhabited the late glacial northeast. Finds of fossil mastodon are common in the Hudson Valley, perhaps because they preferred the forage of marshy valley bottoms, and when they perished, their carcasses became mired in the protective sediments of swampy ground. But aside from an association of human implements with caribou remains in Dutchess Quarry Cave, no large game species have been found within Paleo-Indian sites. Bone of any kind is extremely rare. Either skeletal remains of prey species have not survived, or the big game hunting that appears typical of Paleo-Indians in the far west might have been much more generalized in the east, including perhaps emphasis upon small mammals and aquatic or avian species. Gathered plant foods were probably important, but it is not yet known whether they made up a significant part of the Paleo-Indian diet.

Hunting probably provided the major source of nutrition, and various archaeological indications as well as theoretical considerations suggest that the Paleo-Indian lifestyle involved small, highly mobile groups exploiting very sparsely populated territories in annual rounds, probably following the seasonal availability of wild resources, including the animals upon which they depended.[6] The larger river valleys, like the Hudson, appear to have been favored, perhaps as water routes for movement between seasonal camping areas. In later prehistory, it is clear that the rivers served as important communication links.

The characteristic Paleo-Indian fluted projectile points for dart or spear tips were flaked from fine-grained stones such as flint with extraordinary technical skill. The thinning of the point, which aided hafting and penetration into the prey, was accomplished by the very delicate removal of a large flake from each side, the scar left by the detached flake creating the typical fluted appearance. Use of large and small points (from less than 1.5 to over 4 inches in length) has been thought by some to relate to the size of the game, but it is also possible that other still unrecognized factors explain the varied proportions. Intact and broken fluted points are the most distinctive artifacts, but many other tool types, as well as flaking debris, make up the bulk of the finds recovered from Paleo-Indian sites.

Locations formerly used by Paleo-Indians tend to be elevated, probably for the view they afforded of the surrounding hunting and foraging areas. Fewer than a dozen principal sites are known and available for study, however, and some of these are already badly disturbed. As a result, Paleo-Indians are perhaps the most enigmatic of Hudson Valley peoples. Much remains to be learned about these earliest inhabitants of the region.

When the rising post-glacial seas flooded the Hudson Valley, the present tidal estuary formed. Under modern flow conditions, the tides are felt as far upriver as Troy, and freshwater runoff from the upper Hudson and Mohawk Rivers normally keeps the advancing edge of the salt tongue stabilized somewhere between Yonkers and Newburgh, though more extreme fluctuations do occur and a dilution gradient is always present.[7]

Varied forms of marine life eventually gained entrance to the estuary and established themselves in the tidal channel. Native Americans made repeated visits to shoreline locations during Archaic (7000 to 1000 B.C.) and Woodland (1000 B.C. to European contact) times to collect shellfish.[8] In shallow tidal zones, eastern oysters (*Crassostrea virginica*) and ribbed mussels (*Geukensia demissa*) were common on rocky substrates as far upriver as Peekskill. Within sandy or muddy bottoms in more saline downriver locations lived hard and soft clams (*Mercenaria mercenaria* and *Mya arenaria*), respectively. By weight and volume, the molluscs are mostly shell, and these durable residues were discarded in masses on the river banks. Judging from other regions of the world, especially the Atlantic coast of South America, the dumps could become immense, rivaling some city landfills in size. Though the mounds were built up by constant addition of shell and other artifactual debris, with naturally accumulating soil in varying amounts filling the voids, it is possible that they functioned as more than simple garbage heaps. Some of the shell sites are located at considerable distance from the former river channel, suggesting that there might have been other reasons why the molluscs were carried so far from their collection area. Since the shells in the living bivalve grow incrementally year after year and leave a record of warm and cold season growth like the rings within tree trunks, the recovered shells can often reveal the season of death, indicating which times of the year were dedicated to collecting.[9]

The appearance of shellfish was paralleled by an influx of anadromous fish, such as the Atlantic sturgeon (*Acipenser oxyrhynchus*), the American shad (*Alosa sapidissima*), and striped bass *(Morone saxatilis)*, as well as estuary-dependent species such as bluefish (*Pomatomus saltatrix*) and menhaden (*Brevoortia tyrannus*) that breed in salt water but use the sheltered lower river basin as a nursery area.[10] In view of their heavy exploitation of molluscs, it is unlikely that aboriginal visitors to the Hudson's shores ignored the river's historically rich fishing. Although fish bones are not abundant within shell mounds, their fragility warns against drawing conclusions based upon the absence of evidence. Other bone remains embedded among the shells indicate continued hunting of prey species native to the deciduous forest, such as white-tailed deer (*Odocoileus virginianus*) and wild turkey (*Meleagris gallopavo*).

Many of the shell mounds are gone today. They have either been shoveled into kilns to be reduced to quicklime for mortar production, carted away for agricultural or construction uses, or cleared to make way for development.[11] Nature has also conspired to erase the evidence, as shell-strewn banks made unstable by human interference have suffered from the erosive effects of slopewash.

In the late 1980s, the Hudson River environmental center at Wave Hill in the Bronx was engaged in a program to explore and conserve archaeological vestiges within Riverdale Park, a narrow swath of city land extending along the east bank of the Hudson in the northwestern corner of the borough.[12] The archaeologist in charge, Valerie deCarlo, located areas that had previously been covered by shell, in each of which the accumulation was virtually obliterated, and the surviving remnants were undergoing relentless attack by erosion. Strollers through Riverdale Park can see in the ragged edge of the declivity that descends to the water's edge the signs of ongoing deterioration from the elements. Unfortunately, deCarlo's work was cut short before she could organize a riverbank stabilization effort, but she demonstrated that, among the threats to survival of ancient cultural resources, looting and development sometimes take a back seat to the awesome powers of nature.

2. War on the Hudson River

Our second tour departs during the tumultuous events of the Revolution, but before we leave, I want to call to your attention a significant aspect of Hudson Valley geography. During its evolution, the river endowed itself with special strategic importance by cutting a sinuous channel through a section of the Appalachian mountain fold belt. This complex band of ridges and peaks bisects the lower Hudson and would have imposed a formidable barrier to north-south communication had the river not carved its own passageway. Not only did the Hudson create an easy water route through intervening rugged terrain, it also provided access from the Atlantic coast to the valley of Lake Champlain, which continues northward into Canada. A portage across the watershed boundary between the Hudson and Lake George imposes the only lengthy terrestrial leg of an otherwise fairly continuous water route between New York City and Montreal.

During the Revolutionary War, the Hudson Valley became a critical defense objective for the Continental Army. American military success depended upon unimpeded communication across the river so that New England could maintain contact with the mid-Atlantic and southern colonies. British forces controlled Canada and, in 1776, they fought their way into New York City, which they held for the duration of the war. In mid-1777, a bold tactical maneuver was implemented in the form of a three-way pincer movement intended to put a quick end to the insurrection by dividing the rebellious colonies. Sir William Howe was to advance up the Hudson from New York, while Lt. Gen. John Burgoyne moved south from Montreal through the Lake Champlain corridor. The third component under the command of Lt. Col. Barry St. Leger would leave Lake Ontario and follow the course of the Mohawk River, taking the American stronghold at Fort Stanwix near Rome, New York, on the way. Each army was to converge on Albany, and none expected to meet serious resistance. Had the operation been successful, the colonies would have been split, and the drive for independence might have ended abruptly.

British luck was in short supply, however, and the anticipated military rout of the rebels dissolved into disaster. Howe decided against supporting Burgoyne and sailed south to attack and occupy the American capital at Philadelphia, while Fort Stanwix withstood the siege laid by St. Leger, who was eventually forced to return to Canada. Burgoyne proceeded slowly and confidently toward Albany, unaware that his two columns of reinforcements would not be joining him. Meanwhile, on the American side, Maj. Gen. Horatio Gates prepared for a defense of the lower Hudson Valley by fortifying a battle line at Bemis Heights, an area of high ground just west of the river near Saratoga. From there, his troops turned back two British offensives on September 19 and October 7. Having suffered heavy casualties during both foiled engagements, Burgoyne found himself in a precarious situation. With American forces swelling in number, no source of supplies, no hope of relief, and the road to the south blocked, he initially retreated but soon had no recourse but to surrender. The American victory at Saratoga was complete, and news of the British defeat encouraged other European nations to view America's struggle for freedom more credibly. Shortly afterward, France entered the war as an American ally.

No further British invasion along the Hudson Valley broke the Continental Army's firm hold on the river. Despite the machinations of Maj. Gen. Benedict Arnold in compromising their defenses, the American fortifications on the rocky promontory at West Point kept the British bottled up south of the Highlands. The fort at Stony Point, at the entrance to the Highlands channel, changed hands several times, but even under British control, it never posed a threat to American possession of the north. In this way, the defense of the Hudson River played a major role in the success of the American Revolution and the birth of a new nation.

The Revolution bequeathed a rich archaeological record in the Hudson Valley, and historical archaeologists are increasingly applying the methods of excavation and materials analysis to its study.[13] Important investigations have been conducted at Saratoga and at the 1782-83 winter cantonment of the Continental Army at New Windsor,[14] among other places. During the two centuries since the war, however, many of the most important military sites have been besieged by legions of curiosity seekers. Though not everything has been destroyed, much has been disturbed. Some sites have suffered other indignities that have rendered the archaeological evidence more difficult to interpret or simply impossible to recover.

Excavations conducted by David Starbuck in 1985-86 at Saratoga uncovered little relating to the battle because subsequent occupation of the site apparently obliterated the earlier wartime evidence. His team explored property on Bemis Heights that had recently been acquired by the federally maintained Saratoga National Historical Park. In autumn of 1777, the Woodworth farmhouse and its adjacent barn stood on the spot chosen for excavation. These structures had been pressed into service by Gen. Gates as American military headquarters and its field hospital, respectively.[15] Starbuck located the foundations of both buildings, but aside from the architecture, none of the finds could be dated with certainty to the time of the military action. The artifacts seemed to come largely from the post-war occupation of the farmstead, an interval of reuse that lasted until the old house – and perhaps also the barn – was finally razed in 1829. Survey of the surrounding area failed to detect any of the still undiscovered mass graves known to have been dug nearby to bury wounded combatants the hospital could not save.

Overzealous restoration was the fate that befell the remains of Fort William Henry.[16] This frontier outpost formed the northernmost limit of British control at the start of the French and Indian Wars (1755-1763). It was built in 1755 on the southern shore of Lake George to block French advance along Lake Champlain, but within two years, it was the scene of the most infamous massacre of colonial North America, a tragedy popularized by James Fenimore Cooper's embellished retelling in his 1826 novel, *The Last of the Mohicans*. Following the fort's surrender to superior French forces under the Marquis de Montcalm, Indians allied with the French slaughtered the sick and wounded within the barracks on August 9, 1757 and, the next day, set upon the main garrison of troops and colonials who had been granted safe passage back to British lines. Montcalm subsequently burned the fort to the ground, and the ruins remained fairly well preserved until the 1950s when local Lake George residents proposed to investigate it archaeologically and construct a replica fort on the spot as a historical museum. Excavations conducted between 1952 and 1954 yielded a wealth of structural details and artifacts relating to the life of the soldier at war, but poor documentation, loss of the original excavation report, inadequate curation of the finds, and the permanent modification of the site by the new log fort (completed in 1956) have made the effort far less informative than it might have been.

Several skeletons of massacre victims were exposed in the military cemetery adjacent to the fort, and these individuals remained on display as part of the museum until 1993 when it was decided finally to bury them. Anthropological examination prior to reburial revealed something of the severity of wounds suffered (embedded musket balls, skulls split perhaps by tomahawk, evidence of scalping) the harshness and strain of frontier fighting (herniated disks, amputated limbs) and the haste with which many were laid to rest (without coffins and probably without coats, which were doubtless needed by the living).

One Revolutionary War site that has proved most revealing is Mount Independence, a flat hill overlooking the eastern shore of Lake Champlain opposite Fort Ticonderoga on the west. The Continental Army occupied both the hill and fort at the start of the war in order to block an invasion of the colonies from Canada. American forces were successful in deflecting the first British advance under Sir Guy Carleton in October of 1776, but troop strength was too weak to resist the next year's expeditionary force under John Burgoyne, who forced the abandonment of Ticonderoga and Mount Independence in July of 1777 on his fateful march to Saratoga. Though the site fell to Burgoyne, it has managed to survive relatively unscathed the depredations of souvenir hunters. Excavation has only begun to reveal hitherto unrecorded information about the quartering, health care, and other aspects of daily life in the early years of the war.[17]

Many of the most informative discoveries concerning the Revolution come from the lower echelons of army life. Buried debris informs most directly about the lot of the common soldier, a subject that history has tended to neglect for want of firsthand sources. Michael Cohn points out that some of the artifacts found on military sites indicate the presence of women and children accompanying the soldiers.[18] Objects with uncertain connections to troops in the field might reflect the distribution of attached families. Cohn points out that excavation of many of the forts has demonstrated their generally limited size, providing a vivid impression of what must have been cramped quarters for even a small garrison and bleak isolation in the most forward of lookout points. The artifacts recovered from such forts often betray an origin among the many colonial farms of the Hudson Valley, as not all matériel was government issue. Much of the equipment used by both sides was 'liberated' from surrounding civilians for the war effort, and replacement gear certainly derived from the same source or from dead soldiers, even of the opposing side. War in the 18th century was fought largely during the fair seasons, and excavations at winter troop quarterings have revealed that huts constructed by soldiers to shelter through the cold were not uniformly planned or executed according to regulations but were built using whatever materials could be gotten and assembled using whatever skills the occupants possessed.[19] Archaeologists of the early 20th century also made a unique contribution when they identified among the hundreds of buttons collected within former British campgrounds regimental uniforms from units that had not been posted to the American colonies.[20] Cohn suggests that such discoveries may reveal the presence of officers who had volunteered for combat service in the New World with military advancement in mind.

The significance of many Revolutionary sites has unfortunately made them attractive targets for collectors and, in many instances, shrines to historical tourism. When the disturbances resulting from these activities are extreme, few if any intact deposits remain, leaving little hope of retrieving useful historical information. Archaeologists are reduced to cleaning up the battlefield for the second time.

3. Hudson River Brick Making in the Industrial Age

Our third and final archaeological tour of Hudson River history deals with the fruits of the Industrial Age. The subject is not a site or place of any kind but an object produced in extraordinary numbers from the early 1800s. At that time, and especially following the disastrous New York fire of 1835, bricks became the fire-resistant building material of choice. The Hudson Valley produced and shipped cityward most of the estimated 30 billion bricks that eventually found their way into urban construction. As a consequence, many New Yorkers live and work amidst a sea of bricks, which represent the Hudson River itself, in multiple personification, serenely overseeing the bustling drama from their perches high upon urban canyon walls.

Most find in brick masonry a rustic simplicity and a warm familiarity, but little else to hold the attention. Bonding patterns break the monotony somewhat, but as a subject for closer scrutiny, the humble brick seems at best mildly sedative. After about 1850, however, most bricks entering the urban market were impressed, or branded, with the names or initials of the entrepreneurs whose great yards fueled the housing boom of a burgeoning New York City. Their craft turned the Hudson Valley into one of the most important brick producing regions of the world. To many amateur enthusiasts, the branded bricks have become items of sufficient historical interest that they themselves have bonded together into organizations[21] and individually amassed large collections. In addition to satisfying their urge to accumulate, brick collectors have assembled a wellspring of archaeological information bearing upon the technology and commerce of one aspect of the building materials trade.

The main historical outlines of the brick making business in the Hudson Valley are well known, and detailed information exists for many of the principal brickyards.[22] Early 19th century firms emerged mostly in the lower Hudson, many located on the huge clay bank of Haverstraw and Grassy Point in Rockland County. The early corporations were typically unstable partnerships among a limited number of landowning families, who formed and dissolved their cooperative ventures as new opportunities arose. The invention and gradual improvement of brick making machines at mid-century boosted production rates, and by the late 1800s, a number of companies that had moved beyond the Highlands into the northern Hudson had grown to enormous size. The huge output from these manufacturers could still be brought cheaply and efficiently to the city market by sloop or barge.

John C. Rose built the biggest and most famous Hudson River brick company.[23] He was a small-scale brick maker and boat builder in Haverstraw until 1883, when he bought riverside claylands just north of Newburgh. The place would eventually be called Roseton in deference to the astonishing size of his establishment. At the time of his death in 1897, his Rose Company was the largest in the valley, and millions of bricks impressed with the familiar ROSE brand had gone into thousands of city buildings. His son, John B. Rose, assumed control of the company, organized the Hudson brick makers into an industrial association, and eventually became a state senator. The Rose yard suffered a sudden, and to many a shocking, financial collapse in 1919 as a result of a declining market.

Other brick making families entered the industry as entrepreneurs from other businesses. The Cuban Jova family, for example, earned substantial wealth by shipping sugar to the U.S. from the Caribbean. Juan Jacinto Jova was the family's New York City representative, and around 1880, he bought a mansion built on claylands just north of Roseton.[24] Using family capital, he began exploiting the clay bank in 1884, more or less in step with Rose's operation to his south. By 1888, he was the sixth largest brick producer in the valley. The first Jova brand used the maker's initials, and bricks impressed with JJJ became nearly as common in city construction as those of Rose's company. In 1895, the shipping business failed, and Jova moved permanently to Roseton to continue brick making. His sons took over the company and modernized production in the 20th century, changing the brand to JOVA and JMC, for Jova Manufacturing Company. The Jovas finally sold out in the 1960s, turning over their land to Central Hudson Power & Light.

The peak in brick production was reached between 1890 and 1910, but market demands dropped and the industry began a slow decline shortly afterwards. The first signs of ill health came in the 1920s, when housing expansion in New York City's outer boroughs turned to wood frame architecture, thereby dealing a blow to brick sales. The rise of iron and concrete architecture may have reduced further the demand for brick in succeeding decades. Ultimately, those brickyards that managed to survive through World War II suffered the coup de grâce in the establishment of new construction standards recommending the use of brick produced by the stiff mud process for all weight-bearing applications. Stiff mud entailed the extrusion of relatively dry clay under high pressure through a rectangular die, the emerging bar being wire-cut at appropriate intervals to form individual bricks. The dryness reduced internal porosity and, when the bricks were fired, resulted in a product with greater compressive strength. Hudson River clays were dug from wet deposits along and beneath the river. Their water content was too high for the stiff mud process, and consequently, a soft mud process had traditionally been used in which a plastic mixture of clay, sand, coal residues, and water was forced into a wooden mold and turned out on a prepared yard surface to dry. Higher porosity after evaporation of the water and occasionally uneven firing were eventually seen as undesirable, thereby rendering these bricks less competitive.

Hudson River brick making underwent a "near death experience" in 1979 when the next to last major brickyard, the Staples Company of East Kingston, closed. The remaining yard survived, however, and continues to function today. The Powell & Minnock Brick Company of Coeymans, having begun production in 1907, still produces the standard soft mud product under the P&M brand in addition to extruded bricks fashioned from the Mount Marion shale quarried several miles away.[25]

As old housing stock gives way to new, many of the early brick structures are disappearing. Bricks from houses demolished through urban renewal often find their way back into other buildings as patches or secondary repair. Despite this displacement, the history of brick making can still be read in part from an analysis of the bricks themselves. In the footsteps of many amateurs, I have assembled a large brick collection covering manufacturers in New York, New Jersey, and Connecticut. Over 1300 specimens are currently archived, ranging in age from the first yellow bricks brought to New Netherland as ballast in Dutch West India Company ships to the last ones produced in the Hudson Valley after World War II. The collection, housed at Fordham University in the Bronx, is intended for historical research.[26] As of 1996, several hundred of the branded bricks have been chemically assayed using powder samples obtained with a drill. Bricks produced at the same locality using similar clays and tempers tend to show similar chemical profiles when their quantitative results are compared by computer. In contrast, the profiles of bricks made at different localities are usually dissimilar. It has thus been possible to match compositional profiles to discover where a particular brick was made. When the chemistry of an unknown brick closely resembles that of bricks from a known manufacturing locality, the convergence of elemental fingerprints suggests that all came from the same place. Using this method, we can ascertain the source of bricks with unfamiliar brands or those produced prior to 1850 that were never branded with an identifying inscription. If the brick was recovered from its original building site, then both the source and destination can inform about the lines of procurement and the dynamics of transport that must have linked them together.

One archaeological problem solved using brick chemistry occurred in the course of excavations at the Rose Hill Manor, a historic house built sometime around 1694 and demolished in 1896. The site, located on the Bronx campus of Fordham University, is in the process of exavation under my direction with the sponsorship of the university and The Bronx County Historical Society. Clearance of the east wing revealed evidence of modification dating to the mid-1850s that involved the construction of a new trough-shaped brick cistern in the crawl space beneath the first floor. Loose bricks as well as some still cemented within the cistern masonry revealed a faint brand in the style of the earliest known examples of the 1850s.

The first brands were produced by carving the inscription legibly into the bottom of the brick mold so that the clay filled the grooves of the letters when it was introduced. As the green brick was dumped onto the yard surface to dry, it retained a mirror image of the impression--that is, the brand emerged backwards on the brick.[27] The cistern bricks were impressed with a reversed brand that spelled out the name REID followed by a five-pointed star. Like the earliest brands, the letters were displayed across the short dimension of the brick face. Shortly afterward, inscriptions were carved backwards so that the brand would be legible, and the brand was reoriented to the brick's long dimension. After 1880, the familiar rectangular recess, or "frog," was initiated to save clay, frame the brand more prominently, and key the mortar more effectively.

Documentation is spotty for the initial phase of 19th century commercial production. Little is known about the complicated business affairs of the early brick making firms, and still less is known about the earliest brands, innovated for advertising purposes in an increasingly competitive market. No REID inscription could be found in any of the brand lists that had been compiled by collectors, so no clues to the identity of the manufacturer and the location of his yard were available.

When several REID specimens were chemically analyzed, the elemental profile appeared to match that of other bricks made in Haverstraw, one of the early centers of brick manufacture. This proved to be the key to tracking down Mr. Reid. The U.S. census for 1850 listed only one individual named Reid in all of Rockland County. The census taker described Patrick Reid as a 24 year old Irish immigrant engaged in Haverstraw as a laborer on a brickyard. The most plausible explanation for the existence of bricks with his name impressed into them seemed to be that Reid had done what individuals are known to have done later in

Four bricks from different periods of Hudson Valley brickmaking:
(A) & (C) late 19th century bricks produced by the
Jova and Rose yards in Roseton, north of Newburgh;
(B) early industrial brick produced by Patrick Reid
of Haverstraw, ca. 1850;
(D) colonial brick from the Treason House,
West Haverstraw, ca. 1770.
Courtesy of the author.

the century, namely, he engaged in speculative entrepreneurship by leasing idle brick making machines (probably on the yard of his employer) and outputting bricks in his own molds with his own identifying brand.

Patrick Reid is attested as a brick worker in the federal census of 1850, but he is absent from the rolls of the state census in 1855. During his short-lived business enterprise in Haverstraw, he must have left a small opus of work, the only known examples of which are in the Rose Hill cistern. Chemical sourcing thus helps track down the origins of bricks with uncertain brands by pointing the way to the correct geographic locality. Census records can take it from there. It remains to be determined whether Reid was in any way instrumental in bringing about the widespread use of brick brands, and how common it was for individuals like him to undertake risky entrepreneurial ventures at the dawn of the great age of Hudson River brick making.

Bricks produced prior to the use of brands – that is, pre-1850 – are another story. Elemental profiles can still pinpoint a source area, but the bricks do not drop a name or set of initials that can be tracked by census to their maker. (One can, of course, determine from census tracts how many potential producers worked within the indicated geographic locality). The commercial distribution network can still be traced as long as the bricks can be connected to the houses in which they were originally used.

Some historic Hudson Valley specimens in the collection, unbranded English colonial bricks with typical dimensions of about 8x4x2 inches, come from the notorious Treason House, formerly of West Haverstraw, New York. Built about 1770, the house was owned by Joshua Hett Smith during the Revolution. In 1780, Gen. Benedict Arnold met British Maj. John André there to supply plans intended to betray West Point and deliver control of the Hudson River to the army of King George. The plot – and Maj. André – died shortly thereafter, but the house lasted well into the 20th century. It was finally torn down to make room for an extension onto the Helen Hayes Hospital.

Several remnant bricks from the Treason House now reside in the Fordham brick archive, and though two have been analyzed chemically, the results are as yet equivocal. One produced an elemental profile that so far matches nothing else. Conceivably, this sample included an odd impurity that skewed the assay. The other Treason House brick appears chemically quite similar to a brick bearing the well-known DPBW brand indicating manufacture by the Dennings Point Brick Works that began operations in 1881 on the Dennings Point peninsula at Beacon. One might suppose that a West Haverstraw house could have obtained all the bricks it required from the abundant clays of the nearby Haverstraw riverfront. The, albeit meager, compositional evidence obtained so far suggests that the bricks may have been shipped some 20 miles downriver from an as yet unknown late colonial brick maker working clay banks on the northern side of the Hudson Highlands. Perhaps the price was better or the social contacts were closer upriver, or perhaps brick production in Haverstraw was still undeveloped. Further sampling will be required to confirm this provenience, but the only way such an identification can be made is by entering the unseen world of atoms and molecules through the methods of materials analysis.

Summary

Our archaeological history tours of the Hudson Valley are now concluded. I hope that the site seeing has demonstrated to you how we can read about the past from unwritten sources. Archaeological evidence adds substantially to traditional historical narratives by divulging new stories and confirming or correcting old ones. Conducting archaeological research is difficult, however, not only because the endeavor is expensive, laborious, and exacting, but also because the remains rarely escape human or natural interference. In general, we do not take care of the archaeological record beneath the ground to the same extent that we care for the historical record ensconced in libraries and archives. Buried sites can be as priceless and revealing as the oldest and rarest of newfound documents, so if we prize our papers because of the wisdom they contain, we ought to assign equal value to material remains that also hold historical truths reflecting upon our cultural heritage. We cannot act otherwise and still claim to live by our own philosophical principles.

NOTES

1. I have had the benefit of guidance from a few archaeological "tour leaders" more experienced in certain aspects of the river's history. I acknowledge with appreciation the comments provided by Eugene Boesch, Michael Cohn, Sid Horenstein, and David Starbuck.

2. Funk, R.E., "Early cultures in the Hudson drainage basin," in *Amerinds and Their Paleoenvironments in Northeastern North America,* edited by W.S. Newman and B. Salwen, pp.316-332. Annals of the New York Academy of Sciences 288, New York, 1977; Eisenberg, L., *Paleo-Indian Settlement Pattern in the Hudson and Delaware River Drainages.* Occasional Publications in Northeastern Anthropology 4, Department of Anthropology, Franklin Pierce College, Rindge, New Hampshire, 1978.

3. McNett, C.W., Jr., B.A. McMillan, and S.B. Marshall, "The Shawnee-Minisink site," in *Amerinds and Their Paleoenvironments in Northeastern North America,* edited by W.S. Newman and B. Salwen, pp.282-296. Annals of the New York Academy of Sciences 288, New York, 1977.

4. Funk, R.E., G.R. Walters, W.F. Ehlers, Jr., J.E. Guilday, and G.G. Connally, "The archaeology of Dutchess Quarry Cave, Orange County, New York," *Pennsylvania Archaeologist* 39/1-4 (1969): 7-22; Funk, R.E., G.R. Walters, W.F. Ehlers, Jr., "A radiocarbon date for early man from the Dutchess Quarry Cave," *Bulletin of the New York State Archaeological Association* 46 (1969):19-21.

5. Sirkin, L., "Late Pleistocene vegetation and environments in the middle Atlantic region," in *Amerinds and Their Paleoenvironments in Northeastern North America,* edited by W.S. Newman and B. Salwen, pp.206-217. Annals of the New York Academy of Sciences 288, New York, 1977.

6. Ritchie, W.A., *The Archaeology of New York State,* rev. ed. Harbor Hill Books, Harrison, New York, 1980.

7. Darmer, K.I., "Hydrologic characteristics of the Hudson River estuary," in *Hudson River Ecology; Proceeding of a Symposium,* edited by G.P. Howells & G.J. Lauer, pp.40-55. Printed by the New York State Department of Environmental Conservation, Albany, 1971.

8. See Claassen, C., ed., *Dogan Point: A Shell Matrix Site in the Lower Hudson Valley.* Occasional Publications in Northeastern Anthropology 14, Archaeological Services, Bethlehem, Connecticut, 1995.

9. Abraham, J.F., "Data from shells: Theory in search of a method," in *The Archaeology and Ethnohistory of the Lower Hudson Valley and Neighboring Regions: Essays in Honor of Louis A. Brennan,* edited by H.C. Kraft, pp.35-44. Occasional Publications in Northeastern Anthropology 11, Archaeological Services, Bethlehem, Connecticut, 1991.

10. Clark, J.R., and S.E. Smith, "Migratory fish of the Hudson estuary," in *Hudson River Ecology: Proceeding of a Symposium,* edited by G.P. Howells & G.J. Lauer, pp.293-319. Printed by the New York State Department of Environmental Conservation, Albany, 1971.

11. See Ceci. L., "Shell midden deposits as coastal resources," *World Archaeology* 16/1 (1984):62-74.

12. DeCarlo, V., "Public archaeology in Riverdale Park,"*The Bronx County Historical Society Journal* 33/1 (1996):13-20.

13. See Fisher, C.L., editor, *Symposium on Archaeology of the Revolutionary War Period. Northeast Historical Archaeology* 12 (1983); Starbuck, D.R., editor, *Military Sites of the Hudson River, Lake George, and Lake Champlain Corridor.* Adirondack Community College, Queensbury, New York, 1994.

14. Principal reports on these excavations are unfortunately unpublished. Campaigns at the Saratoga Battlefield were conducted by Robert Ehrich (1941), John Cotter and Edward Larrabee (1957-64), Dean Snow (1972-75), and David Starbuck (1985-1986). Reports are kept on site at Saratoga by the National Park Service. Charles Fisher's investigations in the early 1980s at New Windsor are on file at the Bureau of Historic Sites, New York State Department of Parks, Recreation, and Historic Preservation.

15. Starbuck, D.R., "The American headquarters for the Battle of Saratoga," *Northeast Historical Archaeology* 17 (1988):16-39.

16. Starbuck, D.R., "A retrospective on archaeology at Fort William Henry, 1952-1993: Retelling the tale of *The Last of the Mohicans,*" *Northeast Historical Archaeology* 20 (1991):8-26.

17. Starbuck, D.R., "Archaeology at Mount Independence: an introduction," *Journal of Vermont Archaeology* 1 (1994): 115-126; "The general hospital at Mount Independence: 18th century health care at a Revolutionary War cantonment," *Northeast Historical Archaeology* 19 (1990):50-68.

18. Cohn, M., "Evidence of children at Revolutionary War sites," *Northeast Historical Archaeology* 12 (1983):40-42; Calver, W.L., "Children's toys found in Revolutionary camps," in *History Written With Pick and Shovel,* by Calver, W.L., and R.P. Bolton, pp.236-39. New York Historical Society, New York 1950.

19. Howe, D.E., "The archaeological investigations of 18th-century temporary military shelters," in *Archaeology in Fort Edward,* edited by D.R. Starbuck, pp.38-59. Adirondack Community College, Queensbury, New York, 1995.

20. Calver, W.L., "The British army button in the American Revolution," in *History Written With Pick and Shovel,* by Calver, W.L., and R.P. Bolton, pp.95-108. New York Historical Society, New York, 1950.

21. In the U.S., the International Brick Collectors Association, or IBCA, is the largest and most active amateur group.

22. O'Connor, R.P., *A History of Brickmaking in the Hudson Valley,* Ph.D. dissertation, University of Pennsylvania, Philadelphia, 1987.

23. *Ibid.* pp.292-298.

24. *Ibid.* pp.288-289.

25. Communicated by Mr. Greg Thomas, plant manager, Powell & Minnock Brick Company.

26. Gilbert, A.S., R.B. Marrin, Jr., R. Wines, and G. Harbottle, "The New Netherland/New York brick archive at Fordham University," *The Bronx County Historical Society Journal* 29/2 (1992):51-67.

27. DeNoyelles, Daniel, *Within These Gates.* Privately published, Thiells, New York, 1982.

West Point

59

Sunnyside

Hudson River Architecture

THANK YOU very much. Before saying anything about the architecture of the Hudson River Valley, I'd like to hold up a copy of the publication that the Landmarks Preservation Commission prepared when the Riverdale Historic District was designated an official historic district of New York City, six years ago. Titled *Riverdale, the First Romantic Suburb*, it will be out on the table for viewing.

What I've done in preservation and in studying the Hudson River started out as a philosophy, so that it fits in to a certain extent with what we're talking about here today.

We had bought an old carriage house down along the river about ten blocks south of here and it suddenly occurred to me that the whole neighborhood was really very beautiful. Yet, I couldn't find out from anybody when that house had been built or how old it was, and I decided that I would pursue this. Though not an architect, I am in a family of architects: my father-in-law was a Fellow of the American Institute of Architecture, I have a son who is an architect, and my wife is a great student of architecture as well as art history. Originally, I was told that the carriage house was from the Edwardian Era, built right after the 1900s. I then found out that it was actually constructed in 1852, at the height of the romantic revolution when people like Byron were writing poetry and Sir Walter Scott was writing romantic novels, all having to do with the Gothic Revival.

If you walk to the front of this room in the Administration Building of the College of Mount Saint Vincent and look out, you'll see one of the best examples of the Gothic Revival in the United States, Fonthill, which was the original private residence on this property when it was owned by Edwin Forrest, one of America's great actors of the 19th century. The residences along the Hudson River have varied a great deal along with the forms of transportation. That worked together because the way people lived and moved about changed at the same time. These can also be symbolized by a red brick such as we were looking at.

Red brick in the United States is the keystone – the material of which the American Georgian houses for the most part were built. You ride around and see in old towns, or even in the Colonial townhouses in New York City, that they are red brick structures with white window sashes and with white around the doorway, very often with a fanlight over the front door. That, of course, is typically Georgian.

Some of the difficulties in describing architecture, especially over the last 150 years, can be viewed in this building, which is a landmark, just by asking you to look around a little bit. You see that there are two rows of columns holding up the ceiling. They are undoubtedly weight-bearing columns here and they're not of any known style. They're not Doric or Ionic or Corinthian, they're a composite style, which was very popular in the 19th century. The columns are a Neo-Classical element, but if you look over at the windows, you'll see another composite. You have what are known in architecture as the Ten Commandment Windows, the two double tablets which is an Italianate style. Above them, you have a round window, which takes the Italianate style and makes it Gothic, and you have it all inside a Roman arch. I would be at a loss as to how to describe the window exactly, but it is an Italianate window with Gothic elements. The other windows with the simple chattel arch over them are Roman, so that we have the Romanesque and Gothic in this room, and also Neo-Classical in the columns.

Just for the fun of it, I walked down the corridor that is on your right as you sit in this room and found it to be very fascinating architecturally because there are Romanesque arches over the entrances to some of the offices, and beneath them, you'll find pure Gothic windows which come up to points. That is the opposite of the Roman arch. They also have stained glass in the windows, which is very typical of mid-nineteenth century. Then, above that, you find a *garde de freize*, those upright things which are French *fleurs de lis*, which are entirely different styles, so that within this room and the corridor, you find so many different elements of the nineteenth century all so beautifully done that it would be almost impossible to say what the interior of this building is. You would have to say, "Well, it's Gothic, and it's partly French, and it's partly Italianate, and it's partly Neo-Classical." It gets to be very fascinating.

Back to the Hudson River, early transportation for the farmers who lived along the river was by Hudson River sloop, which took produce down to Manhattan for sale. I'm going to concentrate more on this part of the Hudson River because that is what all of us know better. The river is so long, going all the way from Mount Marcy down to the New York Harbor and its architectural history is so long and so complex that one talk couldn't possibly encompass it all. In fact, I have to look and make sure what the time is here, because I'm trying to cover 472 years in about ten minutes, which isn't an easy thing to do.

The Hudson River Valley during the colonial era was a farming area. But it was very different from the farming area where I grew up in New England. New England farms were small and owned by a single family who were trying to make a living or trying to get wealthier on a modest farm. The Hudson River Valley was very different. As you all know, it was settled under the Dutch starting in 1609 and running to 1664. This was a very important fifty-five years because at the end of that period, the Dutch were no longer in power yet they all stayed here. The Van Cortlandt family for example were still extant and living on their property into this century, which is a remarkably long span of time.

In the Hudson River Valley there were great patroons who had enormous tracts of land. As a result, farming was very different from that in New England. There would be one enormously rich person, at least in the terms of those days, living in a manor house like Van Cortlandt Mansion, or Rose Hill Manor. You had the Van Cortlandt Manor up in Croton, the other one in what is now The Bronx, and the Philips (originally Vlipps) family house in Claremont further up the river. These people had enormous properties.

The Dutch West India Company sold, or gave, large tracts of land only to people that they knew would be able to run them properly. In each area there were a number of small farmhouses and then one mansion such as the Van Cortlandt Mansion which, unfortunately, was not built in Dutch Colonial times. It was built under English rule so it has some English overtones to it. If you look at that mansion, you'll find it really is a Georgian house but it's made of a greyish-tan stone which is not what we think of as Georgian.

The farmhouses naturally have almost all disappeared. If you want to see the Dutch farmhouse style, the best place to go is the Dyckman House in northern Manhattan, at 204th Street and Broadway. Although built in 1783, the building is a good example of what a Dutch farmhouse looked like, and it is in excellent condition.

I want to point out an amusing thing to anyone who is interested in the architecture to be found in the Hudson River Valley, which is that the word *colonial* is used in real estate ads to mean "absolutely almost anything." I looked up ads and found: "This is a colonial house, $500,000." I looked at it and asked, "What colony was that from?" *Colonial* merely means something that was built in an area when that area was a colony. It was a Dutch colony for 55 years and an English colony from 1664 to 1776, and it hasn't been a colony since then, so what the word *colonial* means is impossible to figure out.

When the colonies won the revolution, they wanted an All-American style which would be very different from the Georgian, so they developed the Federal style, which was the first truly American style but which was really just an adaptation of Georgian. That was the red-brick style with the white window sashes, which went on into the early 1800s. Although we cut ourselves off from England and didn't want to be British at all, our styles unfortunately still came from England. Then Greek Revival started. You can still see the style in many banks. Southern plantation houses all had to install columns with a pediment over them in order to look like Greek temples. The height of this style was around 1825 to 1850.

At that time, there were also people living in very simple houses. We were running on two tracks, one for the manor houses and one for the simpler houses where people lived who were just trying to make it, the way most people live. That went on until the 1840s or 1850s and then, suddenly, John Ruskin in England discovered Gothic. That was the era of houses like Fonthill out here, the magnificent castle. People wanted very romantic houses and John Ruskin wrote a book that stated, "No house made of white wood is acceptable. These stand out in an ugly way from the landscape. The houses must be muted colors that fit into the landscape. Make them out of stone or dark wood and make them in the Gothic style, which is the only way to build." So people began building houses with Gothic windows and with towers and turrets and with crenellations along the roofs and anything that they could afford in order to look Gothic and be very stylish.

There aren't too many examples of Gothic left, but a fine example around Riverdale is just south of 242nd Street. The Dodge mansion on the Dodge estate, called Greyston, is a Gothic house and oddly enough, it's Persian Gothic, as there are a few Persian elements to the design. Also, there are two really very perfect Gothic churches in this area, both on Henry Hudson Parkway, one at 249th Street on the west side and one at 252nd Street on the east side. These are the Riverdale Presbyterian Church and Christ Church (Episcopal), respectively. These two churches were built in the mid-nineteenth century. Even Gothic churches, however, are capable of being destroyed or being replaced. In Riverdale, St. Margaret's was a Gothic church, and it was taken down and replaced by a contemporary building 10 to 15 years ago because it was so hard to heat and inconvenient to use.

Some of these Gothic houses and structures of that sort were changed again in the late 19th century into the Second Empire style, which is a style with mansard roofs. Outside there's sort of a flat roof and then a sort of sloping roof and then suddenly a very steeply pitched grey slate roof, called a mansard. There's a perfect example on this property: If you go over to 261st Street on the southeast corner of the College of Mount Saint Vincent, there's a perfect little Second Empire building. There aren't too many of them left.

There were two estate houses nearby that were really built in that style, the more important one being Wave Hill. Wave Hill was made into a Second Empire Victorian house. It had originally been a Greek Revival house of the 1840s, which was changed in the late 19th century into one of the Second Empire houses, with a big *porte cochere* over the front door so the family could be picked up in the family coach without getting wet. Then it was changed again in the 1920s into Georgian, which was going way, way back. It had gone from 1825 to 1890, then in the 1920s, it was suddenly thrown back to an 18th century style, so it's evolved quite a bit. The Gothic Revival and these other styles highlight the highest point of the Hudson River architectural development.

Transportation for the elitist estates in Riverdale was the railway train, which came through in 1849 and made it possible for people after 1849 to live in the great manor houses and travel easily to downtown Manhattan. Around the turn of the century, the pressure for transportation became so great that the subways were built, and people could move around in such enormous numbers that they started building apartment houses. One has to wonder – it's still a philosophical question – if you build big apartment houses on the river, large numbers of people can get wonderful air; they can get wonderful views because no one can build on the Palisades across the river in New Jersey. If you go down the river on a boat, the more apartments there are, the less beautiful is the view from the river, so you have a philosophical quandary. Is it more important to build lots of apartment houses which are not beautiful from the outside as you go down the river, but are wonderful for the people living in them? I won't offer any solution to that.

NOTES

Outside of the few manor houses of the great families, which were Dutch baroque stone mansions, most of the houses were wooden Dutch farmhouses, low, small, with long sloping roofs and dormers to enlarge and illuminate the upstairs rooms. The Dyckman House is a good example. A perfect mansion of the period is the Van Cortlandt house in Van Cortlandt Park, which really has more of an English style, a simplified Georgian not too different from Dutch, built 80 years after the English took over but almost 30 years before the revolution. Another example is the Valentine-Varian House which was built of fieldstone in 1758 and now is the home of the Museum of Bronx History.

The Dutch and later the English settlements were huge land holdings: the Van Rensselaers up near Albany, the Livingstons along the mid-Hudson, the Philips and Van Cortlandt families in Westchester and what is now The Bronx. The early stone houses in the Dutch style had small diamond-shaped window panes and some are said to have been dug up in Van Cortlandt Park from the era of its first owner, Adriaen Vander Donck. He is said to have built a plantation house for himself in the park and had colonists farming on his lands all the way from Spuyten Duyvil to Croton.

The really typical Hudson River style is that of the mid-19th century, the Gothic Revival and Italianate, which came along after 1825 and knocked out the Georgian style of 1775 to 1825. Much like the Federal style, it had severe four-square red brick houses with white wooden door frames and window frames. The new Gothic Revival or romantic style had lots of fancy gables, a revolt against the severe Georgian style. It had ginger-bread or carpenter Gothic decorations hanging from the eaves and inside the steeply arched dormer windows. Windows had tiny window panes like those of 200 years earlier, and often a tower at the corner, and fancily shaped shingles. This style was called Queen Anne Gothic.

I have a whole book of Andrew Jackson Downing sketches for Gothic villas and houses. The main difference? Not having one floor or two floors, as I had thought, but how many servants were required to run one. A cottage could run on two or three in help. A simpler cottage, done without an architect, for a family of modest means, would be like the famous Edgar Allan Poe cottage on the Grand Concourse. This is an early-19th century simple cottage which, unlike a farmhouse, had little land around it. Were it not for Mr. Poe, who lived there from 1846 to 1849, the cottage would have disappeared early in this century when a wave of apartment building swept the area of the cottage.

There is a fine Italianate house of the Victorian era called STONEHURST at 5225 Sycamore Avenue in Riverdale near 252nd Street. It is stone, with its doorway on the side, and a great round porch, dormers and fine brackets under the eaves.

In recent years the towns along the river have developed along with transportation, meaning the automobile, bus, train and subway. First commuters lived in modest wooden cottages, later many lived in elaborate suburbs, in all kinds of housing styles. Finally we moved into the era of apartment houses, con-dominium complexes, and apartment towers.

Esopus Lighthouse

69

Kykuit

MS. TEMA HARNIK

Historic Hudson Valley

THINK ABOUT what embodies the "identity" of a community, and you will very likely find yourself picturing a historic building, special view, or way of life, highlighted by some marker of local history.

Even if you've only recently moved to the lower Hudson Valley or the metropolitan New York area, you, like most of us, are eager to "inherit" the charm, history, architecture and community stories the moment you hear about them. We come from such a diversity of places, we seek instant roots – and are thus fascinated with the dramatic histories of otherwise quiet urban and suburban spaces. As citizens of historic communities, we join readily in the celebration of specialness of the past.

Some have called it a "sense of place" – that quality of historic presence that pervades Bronx and Westchester neighborhoods, where many 18th and 19th century sites are accessible, visible and waiting to have their stories of progress and development interpreted to the public.

One of the things that enlightens our quality of life is this historic "sense of place" in our communities. In this part of New York we feel an attachment to Henry Hudson's first sightings, to the American Revolution, the Industrial Revolution, the Hudson

River Railroad, the Underground Railroad, and the very development of both the spectacularity of New York City and of a suburban way of life – precisely because our communities have a layered, historical context.

In Westchester we can experience this history walking past 19th-century graveyards such as St. Paul's Church National Historic Site, Eastchester, or Sleepy Hollow Cemetery, Tarrytown, or past old farmsteads such as the Dyckman House in northern Manhattan.

We sense it at the great estates, such as the Bartow Pell Mansion and the Van Cortlandt Mansion in The Bronx, Philipse Manor Hall and John Trevor's Glenview in Yonkers, John Jay Homestead or Caramoor in Katonah, Estherwood in Dobbs Ferry or Lyndhurst in Tarrytown.

We associate beautiful community architecture with famous individuals such as Poe Cottage and Wave Hill in The Bronx, the Draper Cottage and Observatory in Hastings, Mme. C.J. Walker's estate in Irvington or Washington Irving's Sunnyside, Thomas Paine's House in New Rochelle, the Jay Heritage Center in Rye or the Van Cortlandt Manor in Croton.

Many of the places which make history are a far cry from Great Estates – but they are places of identity and special character – including High Bridge, the Square House in Rye, the Elephant Hotel, Somers, the Pound Ridge Museum, The Old Croton Aqueduct Trailway State Park, Ossining's Urban Cultural Park, the Cudner Hyatt House, Scarsdale, Smith's Tavern, Armonk, The Bedford Green or Croton Point Park.

What all of the latter examples have in common is that they are run by private, not-for-profit local historical societies and museums, along with county, city and state parks agencies, and preservation trusts, that abound in every nook and neighborhood of our region.

The work these state-education department chartered organizations do involves collecting, preserving, interpreting and providing access to history for present and future residents and researchers. Sometimes called the communities' attics, they are treasure houses of local inheritances. The treasures these groups preserve and present are usually subtle and not overtly golden ones: 19th-century newspapers and photograph collections, family reminiscences and local business records – a multitude of threads in the fabric of local life.

The objects and the archives of these institutions, in addition to the houses and buildings containing them, are cared for by a cadre of community leaders – stewards and trustees – who care for these inheritances in the Public Trust.

Stephen Weil, emeritus senior scholar at the Smithsonian's Center for Museum Studies, wrote in the April, 1996 *Museum News*: "What each of our institutions contributes to its community derives not from its common denominator, but from its distinctive numerator – from what it alone can contribute to the well-being of a specific group of people in a specific time and a specific place."

Picture it in your mind: the Hudson River or the Hudson Valley: our urban, suburban and even rural mix of communities and neighborhoods oddly skewed and dashed with municipal and county boundaries.

Those of us fortunate to live, study or work in the lower Hudson Valley have become keepers of a layered history – the 18th, 19th and 20th centuries mold, one on top of the other, over a special terrain described and delineated by engineers, naturalists and artists, alike. Among those unpublished observers of the poignant moments of development ushered in in the era between the Erie Canal and the Civil War, was young engineer/ illustrator Fayette B. Tower, who worked in this region on the great twin public works of the 19th century: the Hudson River Railroad and the Old Croton Aqueduct. Coming from Oneida County, upstate, Tower's letters home – written between 1836 and 1842 – give a particularly sharp impression of the region's geography and its residents.

In 1836, 19-year-old Tower wrote his mother from Harlaem (now spelled Harlem): "I do not like the place at all. I was much disappointed in the village of Harlaem. Every House, almost, is a resort for horse jockeys and sporting characters from the city."

By September of that year he wrote home from Eastchester: "I have been hard at work through the meanest country that I ever met with. I have been as far as Bedford in this county – about 40 miles from our starting point, and about 50 miles from New York. We have found a pretty rough country from Harlaem, 30 miles north, and the inhabitants have generally corresponded with the face of the country. . . .

"I have dropped into a great many curious places since I have been on the line – sometimes lodging on feathers . . . sometimes on straw – sometimes on bedsteads and sometimes on the floor . . . . Not withstanding I am obliged to put up with many impositions, I find much in this country which is very interesting. I saw a while ago the house where Washington had his 'headquarters' in the Revolutionary War, and the ground on which was fought the bloody Battle of White Plains. I find some old men who like to sit down and tell the many hardships they endured – the many narrow escapes they had – and curse the 'Tories,' some of whom are now living among them.

". . . . (in making surveys for the railroad), I have had opportunities of seeing and learning much of the inhabitants of the country through which I pass – all the land lying between the Hudson and East Rivers from Harlaem 3 miles north, belongs to the Morrises. There is one – Gouverneur Morris – who owns 1399 acres of land for which he was offered one and a half millions of dollars and refused it. I saw this Mr. Morris last week and I never was more surprised than when I learned he was the man who owned so much property.

"I had occasion in my survey to go to his house. We were at work near the house when there came along a 'six-footer' asking questions about (our work) and saying he had a map of the place which we could have if it would be of any service to us. We supposed he must be one of Mr. Morris's laborers, and didn't feel bound to answer every question . . . asked . . . Presently one of the party asked him if Mr. Morris was at the house. When, to our no small surprise he said, 'I AM THE PERSON.' He had on a buckskin jacket, an old fur cap and his pantaloons tucked inside his cowhide boot legs. His house, which is a large stone one, stands in the midst of a corn field and weeds as high as your head are growing about the door . . . He is not the kind of farmer I should think he would be for a man of his property."

In September, 1838, 21-year-old Fayette Tower wrote from Sing Sing:

"I this morning witnessed the laying of the cornerstone of the dam in the Croton River for the Aqueduct, and I can assure you all of us who were present felt quite enthusiastic – though we had no oration on the occasion . . . or anything of the kind to commemorate (it). . . . There is now water enough in the river to furnish over 60 gallons daily to each of New York City's present inhabitants.

"From this you may see that there will never be a want of water. . ."

Tower's letters home continued to observe and remark on the economic, political and natural wonders of the time:

In June 1839 he wrote of the decision to build the High Bridge over the Harlem River, rather than the Low Bridge the Chief Engineer Jervis thought would be more economical and useful.

"Yet the citizens of New York have suffered the load of some 8 or 10 millions for the construction of the aqueduct, to be increased by the addition of half a million for a little architectural beauty in a place where there is little receptivity for it . . ."

Then in June 1842, as the great reservoir in the site of the present New York Public Library and Bryant Park (Fifth to Sixth Avenues, 40th to 42nd Streets) was being filled with Croton water, Tower recalled how:

"first in the morning John Jacob Astor came to see the reservoir, seated in a very low carriage, so that he could step out without difficulty, though he had grown very infirm with age. His head was bent forward beneath the weight of years, and on being introduced . . . he turned up one eye . . . and remarked, 'I think you ought to make money here.'"

Today, poised at the cusp of the 21st century, we too look upon remaining historic sites and museums as good not only for the soul of a community, but as great for the economy.

Increasingly, communities look at local institutions and monuments with an appraising eye. Economic development – as Astor's comment reminds us – has always been a crucial component to a community's health, and has become the yardstick against which the value of institutions is measured. Historic sites have become the mainstay of the region's tourism industry – bringing financial support to non-profits and contributing to business development by making their communities more attractive places in which to live and work.

Monuments have been a particularly good investment in the past – with over 200 museums and historic sites, the lower Hudson Valley is now heralded as a unique *destination* for people to see and visit.

Lower Hudson Conference is continuing to compile information from our member sites and cultural institutions in Westchester, Putnam, Dutchess, Rockland, Orange and Ulster Counties, in Western Connecticut and in the metropolitan New York area – to help form a picture of the heralded past and the future economic impact and community value of the region's cultural heritage resources. We hope you will join us in reaffirming our appreciation and stewardship of the public trust as embodied in our historic homes, districts, views and special places along or associated with the Hudson River Valley.

Indian Village

77

College of Mount Saint Vincent

MS. MARY SIOBHAN SULLIVAN

What We Say When We Write About the River

I TEACH four writing classes here at Mount Saint Vincent and each one of those meets in a classroom overlooking the Hudson, although two of those classes meet in a computer lab. Following no social science protocols that I know of, I concocted a writing exercise designed to see how many of them would think to mention the river. My first directive instructed them to freewrite about the word water. Freewriting is a kind of brainstorming or free association exercise which permits a writer to ignore the standard rules of writing. Fragments and misspellings are allowed; no thesis statement is required. Freewriting operates on a kind of river principle in that you are not supposed to stop the words from flowing. Even if you stall in an eddy, bubbling over the same obstacle and repeating yourself, you keep your pen moving. My students are not particularly fond of freewriting – although they don't actively resist it. Their expressions were slightly baffled and sure enough, many first sentences began with the claim that there is nothing to say about water.

Although a few students mentioned the Hudson itself, or rivers in general, it was interesting to note that none in the computer lab did. Examples of student writing include the following: "It amazes me every time I look out the window and see

New Jersey right across from me, but still I cannot run over because it is separated by this huge river that looks so peaceful." "I can remember times sneaking across to the River and sitting on the rocks on a sunny day and watching the River flow south." "Imagine life without water – look out of the window over to the Hudson River, or should we just call it the Hudson Valley?" ". . . driving over a bridge in the early morning when the sun is out, pure serenity and peace. It seems tranquil but it's never the same water you are seeing." "Orientation weekend I went crazy when I noticed how close we were to the river. I went down to the gazebos and just stared. I wondered what the other people were doing on the other side of the river." Other associations with water included memories of swimming and ruminations on biology, drowning and pollution. I wanted to know if they imagined themselves as connected to their natural environment or alien from it. A few pieces recognized how our culture, whether television commercials or classroom assignments, mediates our impressions of nature. After rhapsodizing a bit, one wrote, "I don't want to sound like a Deer Park commercial." Another mentioned *The Jungle Book*, still another, Club Med. A few were careful to manipulate the reader's impression: "I'm not saying I'm 'Miss Water Conserver' and 'I'm not a Nature freak.'" Perhaps most were thinking what one student articulated: "Where does she get this stuff?"

A classic paradigm for the study of literature has argued that our Western culture's writing represents the following conflicts: Man against Man, Man against Himself, Man against Society, and Man against Nature. Why should conflict, why should agonistic thinking come first in our imagination? Metaphors about dominating nature are out of fashion these days. The liberal imagination cringes at the emphasis in Genesis on subduing nature, although the biblical notion of stewardship still resonates with many environmentalists. The four classic literary conflicts have been revised in recent years. The foreboding and masculine generic of Man has been replaced by a reference to the self. Ralph Waldo Emerson referred to this entity as the soul: "The universe is composed entirely of Nature and the soul. Soul, self, uppercase Man, the individual – the words for this organism need not be set apart from nature." But the very grammatical structure of our language insists on separation: subject verb object. Thus when I framed a question for writing students about one's "personal relationship with nature," they floundered for something to say until they found an active verb. The first sentences were nearly all definitions – Nature is pure, it is animals. – They appreciated it by and large, although a few longed for peace and relaxation through it. The abstractions of people or man or society were ruining it. The romantic striving to collapse the boundaries, to be "one with nature" has a long American tradition. It belongs to days when territories were unexplored and unexploited. Our culture is in a time of recycling. We don't do it very well yet, but we recognize that all is being used up.

My title, "What We Say When We Write about the River," alludes to Raymond Carver's short story, "What We Talk about When We Talk about Love." Carver's title expresses the frustration of the poet who knows that language is a barrier to pure knowledge of a thing in itself. In this way the poet and the scientist are alike, they share the goal of apprehending an object in its entirety. The poet wants to write love itself, not write *about* the love. The preposition is a barbed wire fence, protecting us from the train tracks and prohibiting us from the river itself. Can we write the river, or must we only try to speak about it? Today I want to begin a consideration of how our language about the Hudson River, and Nature generally, has changed over time. We hear of exploration and development, preservation and restoration, exhaustion and apathy; we still hear hope.

As the early Euro-American explorers, historians, biologists and satirists faced the task of describing the natural world on this continent, overwhelmed and awestruck, they either presented the plainest facts of longitude, latitude and weather, as in Henrik Hudson's logs – or they protested that the sublime beauty escaped the power of their pens. Our perception of the American landscape as raw and savage has been created by writers eager to believe that they were originators of an entirely new culture, that this Nature would speak directly to them, and not through European histories and religions. When Thomas

Jefferson bemoaned the loss of aboriginal peoples, it was the death of their language, and thereby access to a new culture which he mourned primarily. Henry David Thoreau noted of the terrain that "it was matter, vast, terrific. Not this Mother earth that we have heard of." The domestic metaphor of nature as a Mother had to be replaced with more virile language in this land of the ever receding frontier.

As the banks of the Hudson sprouted settlements and towns, as domesticity settled in, the social tasks of the fiction writer could begin. Awe could be replaced by satire, as in this passage by James Kirke Paulding in 1828, from *New Mirror for Travellers: and Guide to the Springs* which begins:

"O it's delightful to travel, Maria! We had such a delightful sail in the steam boat, though we were all sick; and such a delightful party, if only they had been well. Only think of sailing without sails, and not caring which way the wind blows; and going eight miles an hour let what would happen." (*Hudson River Anthology*, p. 9)

Satirical advice on steamship travel manner follows, including a host of ways to be rude to the ladies. He advised his readers,

"Whenever you are on deck by day, be sure to have this book in your hand, and instead of boring yourself with the scenery, read the descriptions which will be found infinitely superior to any of the clumsy productions of nature." (p. 14)

Emerson wondered where the American poet was, with a voice as magnificent as the country. Paulding's passage reflects a refusal to attempt such epic goals. Many travel writers, specialists in the comic sketch like Washington Irving, Nathaniel Willis and George Curtis chose their amateur rank. Theirs is the literature of evasion according to Ann Douglas. The theme of evasion as a particularly American feature in writing was first articulated by Leslie Fiedler.

Fiedler describes the most famous Hudson River hero – Rip Van Winkle, as presiding over the birth of the American imagination; and it is fitting that he "memorialize the flight of the dreamer from the shrew – into the mountains and of our time, away from the drab duties of home and town toward the good companions and the magic keg of beer. Ever since, the typical male protagonist of our fiction has been a man on the run – anywhere to avoid 'civilization.'" (*Love and Death in the American Novel*, pp. xx-xxi) As you may remember, Rip wanders into the Catskill Mountains and sleeps through the American Revolution. His escapist fantasy and his willingness to lose his identity indicate that American hard work and restraint, as preached by Ben Franklin, may get in the way of pleasure.

Writing 15 years after Fiedler, Judith Fetterly expands his recognition of Dame Van Winkle as the unsympathetic character. She represents responsibility, the ugly side of authority, and women readers are expected to agree with all the other women in the village who side with Rip. Rip, after all, has rejected working for profit. Who are the Rip Van Winkles living by the Hudson today? Who are the shrewish wives insisting on the moral imperative of work? And who are the "goodwives" who act as perfect barometers for weather prediction? When Rip wanted to escape domestic confines, he had the mountains.

Born two hundred years after Rip, Sticke, the heroine of *Against Gravity* by Lucy Ferris, (1996), has only the strip malls tucked between Route 9 and the Hudson River. A hundred miles north of Manhattan, the town is an entity that is defined by what is gone. The narrator tells us "her universe has no shape, no over arching construct: I ride on the stream of my life, pulling my past along with me in pieces, jagged and half formed. If I stopped to look for the center of it all, I would surely drown."

A similar despair informs the lives of Francine Prose's *Primitive People*. An illegal immigrant from Haiti works as a nanny for a divorcing couple in Westchester County. All the characters involved long to merge back into their environments, to find the safety of a place they could call home. I mention these two contemporary women writers because their female characters are also on the run. But their options are more limited than Rip's. He wakes up, remember? This difference may have less to do with gender than with history, but if Prose and Ferris are a new kind of "goodwife" looking at the Hudson with their barometers, the forecast doesn't look promising for the flourishing of human lives. Survival, however, seems possible.

A writer's task consists of finding the words to say it, whatever the elusive "it" may be. I came to this table today, prepared to listen not only to the expertise of the panel members (on a topic completely new to me, by the way), but to the language they would choose. I have come with an ear tuned for metaphors. Each of us could generate a number of metaphors using the river to represent something else: origins, change, escape, thought, barriers, conduits, memory, time, even life itself; the list goes on. Yet much of our purpose here has been to talk about the River itself, not to try to interpret what it means. I have been listening to the tenor and tone of the conversation, wondering what proportions would be given to the literal and to the figurative. The language of science, of problem solving and project planning usually insists that we be literal. Yet figurative language has also been praised, in the spirit of Darwin, as an ability to make language adapt itself to changes over time. This split between the literal and the figurative is fundamental to modernism, to the belief that history is about progress and continual improvement.

The poet Elizabeth Sewell wrote in 1960 that we "have almost two languages on our hands . . .'language as poetry' and 'language as science.' (*The Orphic Tongue*, p. 6) She argues that it is widely accepted that "with advancing civilization comes a progress from imaginative and mythological and poetic turns of speech toward the logical, precise, nonfigurative." (p. 8) Yet as Sewell and many other twentieth century writers have recognized, it is a mistake to divide science and poetry, mathematics and words, analysis and synthesis because the act of thinking cannot be so neatly split. As many linguists, psychologists and poets have observed, metaphors inform the way we think. They structure human experience by entailing other metaphors and concepts, and many metaphors are said to arise out of physical experience.

It is clear from today's gathering that our physical experiences of the Hudson are many, accessible not only through direct contact, such as those of you who drive over it and dive into it, but by way of the language of history and science. Because metaphors both illuminate and obscure, my task today has been to remind you to notice what it is you say, when you talk about the river.

Rip Van Winkle

Chelsea Piers

Planning for New York's Waterfront

I THINK it is fitting that I go last because it is a planner's task often to take very diverse elements and to try to fit them together in some kind of coherent whole and particularly to try to come up with a vision that encompasses these diverse elements. It is particularly challenging for us to work on the waterfront of New York City. The City has a 578-mile shoreline. It is bigger by far than any other municipality's in this country and even in the world. The Department of City Planning has responded to this rather daunting planning opportunity, this extraordinary planning opportunity, by coming up with a comprehensive waterfront plan that looks at the whole waterfront. The plan really celebrates its diversity and tries to present a long-term, long-range vision for how the waterfront will balance the needs for environmentally sensitive areas and those of a working port, to provide opportunities for waterfront public access as well as housing and commercial activity.

You have heard a lot of different points of view today and I will try to sum up these things into a vision for the 21st century as to what the waterfront should be: The plan sees the 21st century waterfront as a place that has parks and open spaces, with a lively mix of activities that are within close proximity and to which the communities of the City have easy access. We also see the waterfront as a place where people can again come down and fish and swim and boat, and find clean waters, if Tom Brosnan and his colleagues can continue to get the funding to continue to clean up. We have spent billions of dollars so far and we expect to spend billions more to do the job that needs to be done.

We want to see the natural habitats taken care of, well cared for and restored. This can happen if people like Cathy Drew can continue to work and spread the word through the educational aspects of their work. We also want to see the maritime and other industries that, though they are reduced in size from their heyday only a few years ago, will be well located in the appropriate places along the waterfront. We want to see them thrive in those places. To achieve this we must be able to solve those issues that have to be solved in order to keep them working, such as finding a place to put our dredged material, and finding ways to communicate along the waterways so that we can use the waters again for more waterborne transportation, particularly in the case of the ferries that Dr. Derrick talked about. We hope that the ferries would criss-cross the harbors and the rivers, and that we would be able to interconnect all of the systems, including bikeways and the pedestrian ways throughout the City so that we could help lessen the traffic and the pollution that we have grown to live with.

We want to consider the panoramic water views that we have and the historic places, the sense of places that we have talked about, and see that they can be preserved and restored and made a possible storehouse and heritage of memories of what the waterfront has been. We can carry that heritage on for future generations. We want to provide for the needs of the City for new housing, and provide jobs for people of diverse economic levels, and see that they can be satisfied in safe and attractive surroundings at the water's edge. I said that we have more of a municipal waterfront than any other city in the country and we're lucky enough that 40 percent of that 578 miles is already devoted to parks and mapped parks, whether they be federal, state or city; some 10 percent of it is zoned for industry, but much of that

10 percent is not, at this point, well utilized; and the rest is in low density housing and commercial uses.

So – the comprehensive plan looks at the waterfront as a kind of combination of four different elements: You've got the *natural waterfront*, the *public waterfront*, the *working waterfront*, and the *redeveloping waterfront*. The *natural* waterfront is where all those sensitive ecological areas are that we've talked about today, the areas that include the wetlands and the habitats that you do not think of as being in an urban waterfront but, in fact, as Cathy has pointed out, do exist even in the most built-up sections of the City. The *public* waterfront contains all those places that the citizens of the City and the visitors to the City can get down to; they can take advantage of the open space that's there, the magnificent views that are out over the water, and take advantage of the recreation that is particularly possible at the water's edge. The *working* waterfront includes all of those water-dependent, industrial uses that are the City's heritage. It's what New York City was really built upon as the Port of New York, and these industries are still here and in need of help. Finally, the *redeveloping* waterfront has those areas that are no longer needed for industry or shipping purposes. These vacant lands at the waterfront are well connected back to the upland communities. These areas can offer new opportunities for housing and commercial development and, in that development, can provide for new areas of public access.

The waterfront plan has several components to it: We have a citywide plan that is available. We went and looked at the local sections of the waterfront. We divided the City into 22 local reaches, as we call them, a reach being a nautical term meaning that you sail from here to there – along a reach. Those 22 reaches, then, were put out in borough volumes, so that there is a plan for each borough of New York City. I am holding the plan for the Bronx waterfront. This is available down at the City Planning Book Store, as is the Citywide Plan. In addition, we have produced waterfront zoning for the first time in the City's zoning resolution. We treated the waterfront as the special location that it really is, and developed a portion of the zoning resolution devoted just to the conditions that are unique to the waterfront. Then, finally, we are working now on revising the policies of the Waterfront Revitalization program, which we will take through a public review process and incorporate the elements of the waterfront plan into those policies, and then take that through the Community Boards, the City Planning Commission, and the City Council.

I wanted to talk a little more specifically about this area of The Bronx, which is covered in the plan for *The Bronx Waterfront*. It involves the elements of the *natural* waterfront and the *public* waterfront, primarily. We identify the Hudson River as a significant coastal fish and wildlife habitat. Cathy talked about the numerous species of fish. Up and down the Hudson, on the Manhattan side and the Bronx side, there are a number of outcroppings of wetlands and habitat areas that draw in that edge condition, the kind of richness that she talked about.

We also have in the *public* waterfront, a new element, a new overlay that has come down, and we have joined with the rest of the Hudson River in a compact known as the Hudson River Valley Greenway. For those of you who have not heard about that, it is a State Legislative compact that involves all the counties along the Hudson River, all the way up through Albany and Troy. The Bronx and Manhattan held out for a little while because of some tax ruling; then they changed the ruling so that the State Legislature gives the money to funding on an annual basis. As a result New York City was able recently to join into this compact. It carries with it the mandate to provide a trail for hiking and a bike trail all the way from the Battery in lower Manhattan clear up to Albany along the Hudson River. Now, in Manhattan, much of that trailway is already in place, or in planning in one form or another. There are a few gaps that have to be closed, but those changes are achievable, and it is possible that, in our lifetime, we will see a complete ring around the island of Manhattan as a public access corridor, a kind of emerald necklace, if you will.

The planning that we have to do, really, has to concentrate on The Bronx because, as you know, we are cut off in large measure from the Hudson River on the Bronx side by the railway. In our plan for the Bronx waterfront, we lay out some ideas that at least can form the concept of beginnings of a trailway and bikeway that can come off of the Henry Hudson Bridge, over Spuyten Duyvil, and can come up, join with the local streets, go up Palisade Avenue behind Wave Hill, then, right at the corner of Mount Saint Vincent's, come around the college and join with the Yonkers site. Most of that is in an upland location but there are a few places where you could get down to the waterfront, one of them being right here, and perhaps you will be able to stick around and see that for yourselves on the walking tour.

Mount St. Vincent is one of the few places along the Bronx waterfront where you can actually take a bridge across the railway and get to the water. We hope that in the future that will be made available more often for public use so that people like Tom won't have to sneak in there out of sight of the guards. This area between the College of Mount Saint Vincent and the Henry Hudson Bridge is a very significant gateway and it is really the transition between two distinct regions, the Hudson River Valley region coming down from the north, and the New York City urban waterfront that extends down along Manhattan and then opens up into the Harbor and the Atlantic bight beyond that. This is truly a two-way getaway.

We see this projected trailway as a very important and strategic element in our planning for the future, so it makes sense to concentrate our activities here. We hope that groups like this will continue to meet to discuss the possibilities of the Hudson. It is our aim and hope that the College of Mount Saint Vincent as an institution can begin to establish a sense of locus that would bring together planning and ideas that will really focus on the attainment of bringing people back to the Hudson who will be able to enjoy the resources that the river and waterfront areas have. Establishing a center for increasing the experience of that River is a very good idea. I commend that to you and we will be very glad to work with any group that comes out of this.

West Shore Railroad

Index

Access to the Region's Core
(ARC) study pp.28,29,32
acid rain p.14
Administration Building p.62
Adriaen Vander Donck p.67
Aegean Sea p.xxiv
Albany pp.xxv, 7,44,67,92
America p.35
American Institute of
Architecture p.61
American Revolution
pp.43,44,46,47,71
American style p.65
Amsterdam p.xxv
AMTRAK p.25
Andre, Maj. John p.54
apartment p.66
archaeologist pp.35,37,42,45,
47,48
archaeology pp.36,38,44,
45,46,47
Archaic p.41
architects p.61
Arctic p.xxv
Arnold, Maj. Gen. Benedict
pp.44,54
Arthur Kill p.7
Astor, John Jacob p.75
Atlanta p.23
Atlantic coast pp.41,43
Atlantic sturgeon p.42
Australia p.12
ballast p.51
barge p.49
Bartow Pell Mansion p.72
Battery p.92
Beacon p.55
Bemis Heights p.45
bikeways pp.90,93
bluefish p.42
brick archives, Fordham
University pp.51,55
brick cistern p.52
brick making machines
pp.49,54
brickyards pp.48,49,50,51,
54,55
bridges pp.25,27,30,75,93
British p.44
Bronx County Historical
Society, The pp.vii,51,100
Bronx waterfront p.93
Bronx, The pp.25,42,51,64,
67,71,72,92,93

Burgoyne, Gen. John
pp.43,44,46
buried sites p.55
Burroughs, John p.xxv
Canada pp.25,43,44,46
Caramoor p.72
Caribbean p.12
Carleton, Sir Guy p.46
Catskill mountains p.83
Central Hudson Power and
Light p.50
chemical profiles of bricks p.51
Christ Church p.65
City Council p.92
City Planning Commission
p.92
Civil War p.73
clams, hard and soft p.41
Claremont p.64
clay bank p.49
Clovis and Folsom p.39
coliform bacteria pp.5,6,8
College of Mount Saint Vincent
pp.vii,xix,xxiii,1,62,66,79,93
Colonial townhouses p.62
colonies p.43
Community Boards p.92
commuter rail lines p.24
commuters pp.27,68
computer lab p.79
Coney Island pp.3,5,7
Connecticut p.51
Continental Army
pp.43,44,45,46
Cooper, James Fenimore p.45
Croton Point Park p.72
Croton River p.75
Cuban p.49
Darwin p.84
deciduous forest p.42
Delaware River p.39
Dennings Point Brick Works
p.55
Department of City Planning
pp.89,101
diesel fuel p.26
dissolved oxygen pp.5,6,8
Dobbs Ferry p.72
Dodge Estate p.65
Downing, Andrew Jackson p.68
Draper Cottage and
Observatory p.72
dredge p.8
dredged material p.90

Dutch baroque stone
mansions p.67
Dutch Colonial pp.63,64
Dutch farmhouse pp.64,67
Dutch West India Company
pp.51,64
Dutchess Quarry Cave pp.39,40
Dyckman House pp.64,67,72
East Coast p.14
East River pp.5,7,25,28
East Side pp.7,28,29
Eastchester p.72
eastern oysters p.41
Egypt p.xxiv
Eighth Avenue p.25
electric subway p.24
electric traction pp.24,26
Emerson, Ralph Waldo p.80
English style p.67
EPA Clean Water Act p.14
Erie Canal p.73
Estherwood p.72
estuary pp.1,14
European contact p.41
Europeans p.36
Exchange Place p.24
farms p.35
Federal style pp.64,67
ferries pp.22,23,28,90
ferry terminals p.23
fish pp.6,13,16,42,92
fish kills p.5
fisheries pp.3,4,14,42
floatables pp.2,3,8,14
Fonthill p.62
Fordham University pp.51,100
Forrest, Edwin p.62
Fort Stanwix pp.43,44
Fort Ticonderoga p.46
Fort William Henry p.45
forts pp.35,43,44,45,46
Franklin, Ben p.83
freewriting p.79
freight trains p.26
French and Indian Wars p.45
Gates, Maj. Gen. Horatio
pp.44,45
General Electric Company p.7
Genesis p.80
George Washington Bridge p.27
Georgian pp.62,64,65,66,67
Gilbert & Sullivan p.30
Gothic elements pp.62,63,65,66
Gothic Revival pp.62,66,67,68

Index

Grand Central Terminal pp.22,25,29,30
Grand Concourse p.68
Great Barrier Reef, The p.12
Greater Hudson Raritan estuarine system p.2
Greater New York City Centennial Celebration p.vii
Greece p.xxiv
Greek Revival p.65
Greek temples p.65
Greenwich Village pp.22,24
Greyston p.65
gribbles pp.6,7,13
habitat restoration p.15
Hackensack p.2
Haiti p.83
Half Moon (ship) p.xxv
Harbor estuary p.15
Harbor Survey Program pp.4,100
Harlem River p.75
Hastings p.72
Haverstraw pp.49,52
Helen Hayes Hospital p.55
Hell Gate Bridge p.25
Henry Hudson pp.xxv,14,71
Henry Hudson Bridge p.93
Henry Hudson Parkway p.65
Heraclitus p.xxv
High Bridge p.75
Highlands p.49
highways p.30
historic sites pp.35,48
Hoboken pp.24,28
Holland Tunnel p.26
Howe, Sir William pp.43,44
Hudson and Manhattan Railroad Company p.24
Hudson crossing p.29
Hudson Highlands p.55
Hudson River pp.vii,xix,xxiii, xxiv,xxv,1,2,5,6,7,8,12,13,14, 21,22,23,24,26,27,28,29,30,32, 35,39,41,42,44,48,54,61,62,63, 67,73,80,83,84,92,93
Hudson River architecture p.66
Hudson River barrier pp.21,25
Hudson River Brick Making pp.48,49,50,54
Hudson River center p.93
Hudson River Railroad pp.72,73
Hudson River treatment plants p.5

Hudson River Valley Greenway p.92
Hudson Valley pp.36,37,38,39, 40,41,43,44,45,47,48,49,51,54, 55,61,63,64,71,73,76,92,93
Ice Age hunter-gatherers p.39
Ice sheet, continental p.39
Industrial Age p.48
Industrial Revolution p.71
Institute for Applied Philosophy pp.vii,xx,xxiii, 11,103
intertidal flows p.16
Irish immigrant p.52
iron and concrete architecture p.50
Italianate pp.62,67
Jamaica Bay p.4
Jay Heritage Center p.72
Jefferson, Thomas p.81
Jersey City pp.24,27
Jova Manufacturing Company p.50
Jova, Juan Jacinto p.49
Katonah p.72
King George p.54
Kingston p.50
KOSMOS p.xxv
Lake Champlain pp.43,45,46
Lake George pp.43,46
Lake Ontario p.43
Landmarks Preservation Commission p.61
Lincoln Tunnel p.27
log fort p.46
Long Island pp.30,39
Long Island Railroad, p.25
Lower Hudson Conference of Historical Agencies and Museums pp.76,101
Lyndhurst p.72
Manhattan pp.6,11,12,13,23,24, 25,26,27,28,29,30,63,66,92
manor houses pp.65,66
mastodon fossil,p.40
Meadowlands p.28
Mediterranean Sea p.xxiv
menhaden p.42
Metropolitan Sewage Commission pp.3,4
Metropolitan Transportation Authority pp.23,28,29,30,100
millennium pp.xxiii,32
Mississippi p.xxv

Mohawk River p.41
Montcalm, Marquis de p.45
Montreal p.43
Morris, Gouverneur p.74
Moses, Robert p.30
Mount Independence p.46
Mount Marcy p.63
Mount Marion shale p.51
MTA Metro-North Railroad's Hudson Lines pp.29,30
Museum of Bronx History p.67
Nassau p.27
Native Americans pp.36,38
New England pp.43,63,64
New Jersey pp.2,5,6,21,22,25, 27,28,30,32,51,80
New Jersey Transit pp.25,28,30
New Mexico p.39
New Netherland p.51
New Rochelle p.72
New Windsor p.45
New World p.47
New York pp.2,22,23,24,25, 27,30,35,43,51
New York Central p.25
New York City Comprehensive Waterfront Plan p.101
New York City pp.xix,xxiii, 3,4,16,25,32,39,43,48,49,50, 61,62,89,91
New York Department of Environmental Protection p.100
New York fire of 1835 p.48
New York Harbor pp.1,3,4,28,63
New York Public Library p.75
Newburgh pp.41,49
North America pp.36,45
Old Croton Aqueduct Trailway State Park p.72
Old Croton Aqueduct p.73
ospreys p.7
oyster fisheries p.4
Paleo-Indian pp.39,40,41
Palisade Avenue p.93
Palisades pp.xix,29,66
Paris p.32
Passaic p.2
PATH System pp.23,24,28
pathogens p.8
Pavonia p.24
PCBs pp.6,7,8
pedestrian ways p.90
Penn Station pp.28,30

Index

Pennsylvania Railroad pp.22,25
Pennsylvania Station
   pp.22,23,25
peregrine falcons p.7
Persia p.xxiv
Persian Gothic p.65
pesticides p.2
Philadelphia p.44
Philipse Manor Hall p.72
Pier A pp.12,13
plantation houses p.65
Poe, Edgar Allan p.68
Poe Cottage pp.68,72
Port Authority of New York
   and New Jersey pp.24,28,30
Port Authority Trans-Hudson
   System pp.23,24,28
Port of New York pp.22,91
Powell and Minnock Brick
   Company of Coeymans p.50
projectile points p.40
public waterfront p.91
Pythagoras p.xxv
Queen Anne Gothic p.68
Queens p.25
rail passenger service pp.25,30
rail tunnel pp.22,23,25
railroads pp.22,23,24,25,26,28,
   29,30,68,72,73,93
Raritan Bay p.4
Raritan River p.2
REID, brick pp.52,54
respect for knowledge p.38
Revolutionary sites p.47
ribbed mussels p.41
Rip Van Winkle p.82
River Project, The pp.11,12,
   15,16,100
Riverdale Historic District
   pp.61,101
Riverdale Park p.42
Riverdale Presbyterian Church
   p.65
Riverdale pp.1,65,66
Rockaway Beach p.2
Rockland County pp.2,27,29,
   49,52
Romanesque pp.62,63
Rome p.43
Roosevelt, Theodore p.22
Rose Company p.49
Rose Hill Manor pp.51,54,100
Rose, John C. pp.49,50
Roseton p.49

Ruskin, John p.65
Rye p.72
Saratoga pp.44,45,46
Saratoga National Historical
   Park p.45
scuba diving p.12
Seagate Beach p.7
Second Empire Victorian p.66
Seventh Avenue p.25
sewage discharges pp.2,6,8
sewage treatment plants
   pp.5,14
sewers p.3
Shawnee-Minisink site p.39
shell mounds pp.41,42
shellfish pp.3,41
Sisters of Charity p.vii
Sixth Avenue p.24
Sleepy Hollow Cemetery p.72
sloop p.49
snorkeling pp.12,13
Solomon Islands p.12
South America p.41
South Midland Beach p.7
Spuyten Duyvil Bridge p.25
Spuyten Duyvil p.93
St. Leger, Lt. Col. Barry
   pp.43,44
St. Margaret's p.65
St. Paul's Church National
   Historic Site p.72
Staples Company p.50
Staten Island pp.4,7,39
Staten Island ferry p.28
Statue of Liberty pp.12,13
steam locomotives p.26
STONEHURST p.68
Stony Point p.44
striped bass pp.6,42
Stroudsburg, Pennsylvania p.39
subsidized transit p.24
subway p.68
SUNY p.12
swimming p.14
Tappan Zee Bridge p.27
Tarrytown p.72
terminal moraine p.39
Thales pp.xxiv,xxv
Thames River p.4
thirty first street p.25
thirty-third street pp.24,25
Thomas Paine's House p.72
Thoreau, Henry David p.82
Thruway p.21

Ticonderoga p.46
Tokyo p.32
trailway pp.92,93
transit connections p.27
transit proposals pp.28,29,30,32
transit service p.30
Treason House pp.54,55
treatment plants pp.5,6
Troy p.41
tunnels pp.22,24,26,27
twenty first century pp.32,89
typhoid p.4
Underground Railroad p.72
United States p.62
Valentine-Varian House p.67
Van Cortlandt Manor pp.63,72
Van Cortlandt Mansion
   pp.64,67,72
Victorian era p.68
wading birds p.15
Wall Street p.24
Washington [D.C.] pp.22,23
Washington Irving's Sunnyside
   pp.72,82
water pollution pp.1,3
Waterfront and Open Space
   Division p.101
waterfront park p.15
waterfront plan pp.90,91
Waterfront Revitalization
   program p.92
Wave Hill pp.42,72
West Haverstraw pp.54,55
West Point pp.44,54
West Side waterfront p.17
Westway Corridor p.13
Westchester pp.2,27,71
Western Civilization p.38
Western Hemisphere p.38
wetlands p.4
white-tailed deer p.42
wild turkey p.42
winter troop quarterings p.47
wood frame architecture p.50
wood-boring organisms
   pp.6,7,13
Woodland p.41
Woodworth farmhouse p.45
World Cities p.32
World War II pp.50,51
writer's task p.84
Yonkers treatment plant p.6
Yonkers pp.5,41
zoning resolution p.91

Old Dutch Farm

Hudson River Conference Biographies

THOMAS BROSNAN is a research scientist with 12 years of experience collecting and analyzing water quality data from oceans, estuaries, lakes and rivers. He currently serves as Chief of the Marine Sciences Section of the New York City Department of Environmental Protection. His responsibilities include serving as the technical lead on marine water quality and as manager of the 86-year-old Harbor Survey Program of New York.

CATHY DREW is a marine biologist and an accomplished underwater photographer. She is currently the Director of The River Project. Their mission is to establish an oceanographic monitoring station in the lower Hudson Estuary and an experimental facility to restore an ecologically stressed environment along the Manhattan shoreline.

PETER DERRICK honed his expertise in transportation as a planner and administrator for the Metropolitan Transportation Authority from 1982 to 1996. Dr. Derrick earned his Ph.D. in urban history, writing his doctoral dissertation on the politics and planning of the largest stage of New York's subway system. He is now the Archivist for The Bronx County Historical Society.

ALLAN GILBERT is an Associate Professor of Anthropology at Fordham University where he also serves as Archaeological Director of the Rose Hill Manor Project. He is particularly interested in the Hudson River Valley region as a valuable source of archaeological knowledge about the human past.

ROBERT KORNFELD is chairman of the Riverdale Historic District which borders the Hudson River seven blocks south of the College of Mount Saint Vincent. He is the originator and Chairman Emeritus of the Bronx Borough President's Landmarks Task Force, and co-author of *Landmarks of The Bronx*.

TEMA HARNICK is an administrative consultant for the Lower Hudson Conference of Historical Agencies and Museums. Their mission is to offer programs for institutions along the Hudson River. She has also served as a Guest Curator for the Hudson River Museum.

MARY SIOBHAN SULLIVAN is a literary scholar who served as a visiting instructor of English at the College of Mount Saint Vincent. One of her favorite writing exercises involves free association with everyday sights and words. In this way, the ideas we take for granted begin to sound new.

WILBUR L. WOODS is an architect who has practiced his trade in London, Copenhagen, and New York City. He is currently serving as the Director of the Waterfront and Open Space Division of the New York City Department of City Planning which is responsible for the Comprehensive Waterfront Plan.

Palisades

ELIZABETH BEIRNE

Elizabeth Beirne is an Associate Professor of Philosophy at the College of Mount Saint Vincent in The Bronx, New York, where she also serves as the Director of The Institute for Applied Philosophy. She received her doctorate in philosophy from Fordham University.

THE INSTITUTE FOR APPLIED PHILOSOPHY

As the "mother of all disciplines" philosophy is an integrating and cohesive force. The Institute for Applied Philosophy serves as the vehicle through which the College of Mount Saint Vincent raises the community's awareness of critical issues in our culture. The aim is to provide a forum in which individuals from many fields can focus on shared problems and concerns. To this end the Institute sponsors conferences, publications, lectures, tours, educational programs, and, generally, serves as a resource to the College and the community on issues related to applied philosophy.

JAN L. MUNRO

New York artist Jan L. Munro captures one's interest on several levels. In her three decades of painting, she has achieved a great deal of recognition.

Munro's canvases are often described as pictoral-history because they focus on documenting the lives of everyday people. Whether it is a painting of lower harbor piers or a brick factory, Munro is always working for realism. Each painting is carefully finished to record a story of life in America.

The scenes created for this book are an excellent addition to our conference theme, *The Hudson River: Inspiration & Challenge.*

105